Difficult Conversations

Difficult Conversations

A Toolkit for Educators in Handling Real-Life Situations

Anni K. Reinking

ROWMAN & LITTLEFIELD
Lanham • Boulder • New York • London

Published by Rowman & Littlefield
An imprint of The Rowman & Littlefield Publishing Group, Inc.
4501 Forbes Boulevard, Suite 200, Lanham, Maryland 20706
www.rowman.com

6 Tinworth Street, London SE11 5AL, United Kingdom

Copyright © 2019 by Anni Reinking

All rights reserved. No part of this book may be reproduced in any form or by any electronic or mechanical means, including information storage and retrieval systems, without written permission from the publisher, except by a reviewer who may quote passages in a review.

British Library Cataloguing in Publication Information Available

Library of Congress Cataloging-in-Publication Data
Names: Reinking, Anni K., 1985- author.
Title: Difficult conversations : a toolkit for educators in handling real-life situations / Anni K. Reinking.
Description: Lanham, Maryland : Rowman & Littlefield, [2019] | Includes bibliographical references.
Identifiers: LCCN 2019001604 (print) | LCCN 2019011917 (ebook) | ISBN 9781475845860 (electronic) | ISBN 9781475845846 (cloth : alk. paper) | ISBN 9 781475845853 (pbk. : alk. paper)
Subjects: LCSH: Communication in education. | Teachers—Professional relationships. | School administrators—Professional relationships. | Teacher-student relationships. | Teacher-administrator relationships.
Classification: LCC LB1033.5 (ebook) | LCC LB1033.5 .R465 2019 (print) | DDC 371.102/2—dc23
LC record available at https://lccn.loc.gov/2019001604

Contents

Preface		vii
1	**Communication**	**1**
	What Is Communication?	2
	Communication Models and Theories	4
	What Is Effective Communication?	6
	Important Communication Strategies	7
	Interpersonal Skills	9
	Why Is Communication Important?	10
2	**Technology Communication**	**13**
	Brain Development and Technology	17
	Technology and Family Communication	17
3	**Communication Barriers and Blocks**	**19**
	Communication Barriers	19
	Communication Blocks	23
4	**Difficult Conversations**	**31**
	Instinctual Reactions and Emotions	32
	Learning from Healthcare	36
	Pseudo-Synonyms	37
	Foundational Toolkit	38
	Definitions	39
5	**Toolkit 1: Supervisor/s and Staff/Teachers**	**41**
	Understand Your Role and Know Your Goals	42
	Difficult Conversations	47
	Staff/Teacher to Supervisors	53

6	**Toolkit 2: Colleagues**	**55**
	Staff Meetings	56
	Special/Extracurricular Teachers	56
	Staff and Teachers	58
7	**Toolkit 3: Educator and/or Administrator to Student**	**61**
	Teacher Language	62
	Mutual Respect	63
	Logical Consequences	63
	Understanding Misbehavior	65
	Replacement Behaviors and Social Stories	66
	Culturally Responsive Practice	67
	Discussion	69
8	**Toolkit 4: Student to Student**	**73**
	Class Contract/Class-Made Norms	74
	Daily Journals and Interactions	74
	Problem-Solving	75
	Discussion	76
9	**Toolkit 5: Administrators and Educators to Families**	**79**
	Welcome Back Nights and Home Visits	80
	Parent–Teacher Conferences	82
	Newsletters and/or Websites	83
	Specifics for Administrators	84
	Administrators Preparing Educators	89
	Discussion	93
10	**A Research Study: Education, Technology, and Knowledge Sharing Communities**	**95**
	Literature Review	96
	Significance	97
	Theoretical Framework	98
	Limitations	98
	Methodology	99
	Findings	102
	Implications	104
	Discussion	104
Epilogue		107
References		109
About the Author		113

Preface

This book was designed to be used as a resource. As the author I also recognize that this is a living toolkit that will change over time. However, this is a great starting point for your toolkit as an educator. Why is this topic, a topic about communication, important in the field of education? Many other professions have multiple resources discussing effective communication, more specifically difficult conversations. However, the field of education has close to none. Therefore, this resource should be used as a professional development tool to reflect on and improve professional practice.

In this book there are also "real-life scenarios." While there are no questions associated with each scenario, the goal is to personally or collectively reflect on the scenario. Every scenario is not perfect, but these scenarios are intended to bring life into the strategies.

Chapter 1

Communication

> *Greg Satell (2015) defends the idea that communication is today's most important skill. In summary, he states that communication is needed in every profession, it is bidirectional, and it goes hand in hand with knowledge.*

Communication is key to any relationship. It is especially important to relationships within the field of education. Why? Because communication between and among stakeholders in the life of a student can build or destroy the foundational relationships needed for impactful and transformational educational experiences. Communication—language—is powerful.

But who are the stakeholders? The stakeholders include anyone who interacts with students. Therefore, transformational relationships include family to teacher, teacher to student, teacher to teacher, teacher to supervisor, student to student, and more combinations of those groups. Communication between these stakeholders can be verbal and/or nonverbal; tone and/or body language; words and/or actions. However, regardless of the communication, positive, respectful, and trusting relationships need to be built in order to engage students in the learning process of social interactions and cooperation now and in the future. Overall, trust is the glue for communication and collaboration.

In this chapter, we will develop a common understanding for the overview of what communication is, why communication is so important, and communication strategies or the "how" of communication. Overall, this chapter will build the foundation for the rest of the book. As you read this chapter and the following chapters, keep an open mind and be willing to reflect on the ideas and strategies introduced to impact your profession as an educator, ultimately impacting the lives of students, the future of our nation.

Why is it so important for educators to develop these skills? Other professional fields, including business, medicine, leadership, and beyond, provide multiple resources and experiences for key communication strategies. However, in the field of education, focused depictions and toolkits are few and far between. Therefore, as a place to start our education communication conversation we will use other professions to build our own toolkit for experiences and interactions in the field of education.

WHAT IS COMMUNICATION?

Communication starts in infancy. From the moment an infant is touched for the first time, to when the infant is held, to the way the family or caregivers feed, make eye contact, and interact with that infant—all of this communicates a message to the infant. All these interactions start the trajectory of verbal and nonverbal development of a child, the child's communication process.

Once babies reach a certain age they begin to communicate, which eventually turns into speaking and other forms of communication. Speech communication, along with other forms of it, are learned through observations, interactions, and experimentation. Every message that is conveyed or received requires effort, persistence, reflection, and at times, self-correction. Learning how to speak, learning how to write, and learning about body language to communicate is all part of the process that concludes in the accumulation of communication skills.

In the first few pages of this book, the word "communication" has been referenced several times but could mean different things to different readers. Therefore, to build a common understanding of what communication means, a few definitions will be provided.

The dictionary defines it as "the imparting or exchanging of information or news" and "means of connection between people or places." Other authors who have discussed the idea of communication, specifically in the field of business, define communication as a "two-way process of reaching mutual understanding in which participants not only exchange information, news, ideas, and feelings, but also create and share meaning. In general, communication is a means of connecting people or places" (www.businessdictionary.com, 2018).

Other scholars, such as Pearson and Nelson (2000), have defined communication as the process of understanding and sharing meaning. Wilbur Schramm (1954) defined communication as something people do. He goes on to define communication as a transmitted message that has no meaning unless people put a meaning into the message. What is the meaning the sender is intending and what is the perception of the receiver of the message?

This idea resonates the common saying that a tree falling in the forest does not make noise unless someone is there to hear it fall. The person hearing it fall is putting meaning to the sound, much like a person puts meaning to sounds, motions, or pictures when communicating. While all these definitions have similarities, they also have some differences. Therefore, the common definition we will use in this book will be a combination, specifically designed for the field of education (see "Communication Models and Theories").

Regardless of the definition, communication is just that, communicating with a purpose. The purpose may be perceived in various ways, but there is a purpose. For example, an infant cry indicates a need for a diaper change or a new bottle. Depending on the caregiver and the sound of the cry, the communication may or may not be perceived in the "right" way.

As students and professionals, communication is also needed in collaborative work, such as team or group projects. If team members are not communicating effectively, or are not communicating at all, the work will suffer. However, when everyone on a team learns how to communicate in a respectful, professional, and effective manner, the work and overall environment will improve, resulting in increased productivity and investment in the product.

In order to understand the foundations of communication, one must understand how people relate to each other in different scenarios. Therefore, it is important to ask yourself, "How well do I work with others in a group?" or "How do others perceive my verbal and nonverbal communication when working in a group?" or "What type of worker am I?" Some key characteristics to consider include:

- Honesty
- Sharing of the workload
- Reliability
- Optimism
- Emotional intelligence, which is the ability to be aware and control personal emotions, as well as being able to read or be empathetic to others.

Overall, communication conveys messages and is often defined as body language, tone of voice, and words. However, there is more to communication than just those three components. Communicating includes how we present ourselves and the perceived implicit biases of others: What does your skin color say about you? What do your clothes say about you? What does your car say about you? What do your jewelry, tattoos, or even the music you listen to say about you? What does your accent say about you?

All these things that are part of who you are as a person communicate something to the perceiver. For example, a common bias in society is that people who have tattoos covering their bodies and piercings all over their face are "bad" people who do not have worthwhile information to convey. Additionally, many times society perceives people of color as dangerous. An example of this was illustrated in a news article in April 2018.

> In Philadelphia on a Thursday afternoon two black men walked into a Starbucks. They were waiting for other people to join them and decided to use the restroom. They had not ordered anything because they were waiting for a meeting. Upon seeing them an employee called the police. When the third person arrived, a white man, the police showed up. In a video recording the white man is heard saying, "What did they (police) get called for? Because there are two black guys sitting here meeting me?" The two black men were eventually led out in handcuffs. (Stevens 2018)

Another example is from an ABC News report in 2016.

> In Toledo, Ohio a little seven-year-old girl, who was a self-described "tomboy" was being bullied at school. Her mother reached out to the motorcycle club called "The Punishers." Often motorcycle riders are tough, mean, dangerous, dark, and big men no one should mess with. However, this motorcycle club, made up of service members and first responders, find it their duty to help children who are being bullied. They have become her uncles and show her that there are nice people in the world, regardless of what they look like or what people may say about "people like them." (Clarke, 2016)

When outsiders perceive a person by their appearance in a negative or biased way, future communication is often shut off. This is unfair but needs to be recognized as a potential threat to the communication you participate in with others. This process of judging someone by their outside appearance rather than the content of their character is truly unfair, but it is also real life and is part of the communication continuum.

COMMUNICATION MODELS AND THEORIES

When studying communication, there are several communication models and theories that are used as foundational pieces of scholarship. The simplest and first formal model of communication was designed by Shannon and Weaver in 1949. Their model consists of a sender, a message, a channel where the message travels, the noise, interference, or background noise, and the receiver of the message. However, Shannon and Weaver's model did not consider feedback.

As is evident in current scholarship, feedback is important in the communication loop to ensure the receiver understands the intended message. It is a way to show active listening by providing restatements and clarification messages. This is also a way to provide motivation, to develop and improve performance, and to continually learn and grow as a professional.

Another communication model and theory was designed by Wilbur Schramm, also in the late 1940s. The modifications he added to the original model included the idea of relationships. How does a relationship impact communication? What is the frame of reference for each party? More additions were made through the Public Opinion Process. What is the opinion of each party? What is the belief of each party? What is the attitude of each party? What is the value of each party? (McAnany, 2017).

Each of these questions is important to ask, reflect on, and keep in mind every time communication occurs in any situation. These questions also consider implicit biases, personal experiences, and deeply embedded values.

Finally, Lasswell's communication model, developed around the same time (1948), is also known as the action or linear model. This model is regarded as one of the most influential communication models, specifically in the field of business (Businesstopia, 2018). Laswell's model includes five steps (see Figure 1.1).

Although this model is well regarded, there are also critics of this model. Some critiques of this model focus on its linear nature, which provides no room for feedback or looping back.

While each of the described communication models is important, the model we will focus on in this book will be a combination of the models, including the closed loop model. The closed loop model is where the receiver restates the sender's message to ensure that the information was received correctly. Normally this model is implemented in the training procedures for resuscitation, but it can also be used in the field of education to develop common understanding (ACLS, 2018).

The model we will use is in Figure 1.2 and will be defined as the Education Communication Model. This model is best used in education settings with

1. Who (Sender)

2. Says What (Message)

3. Channel (Medium or Mode)

4. To Whom (Receiver)

5. Effect (Feedback).

Figure 1.1.

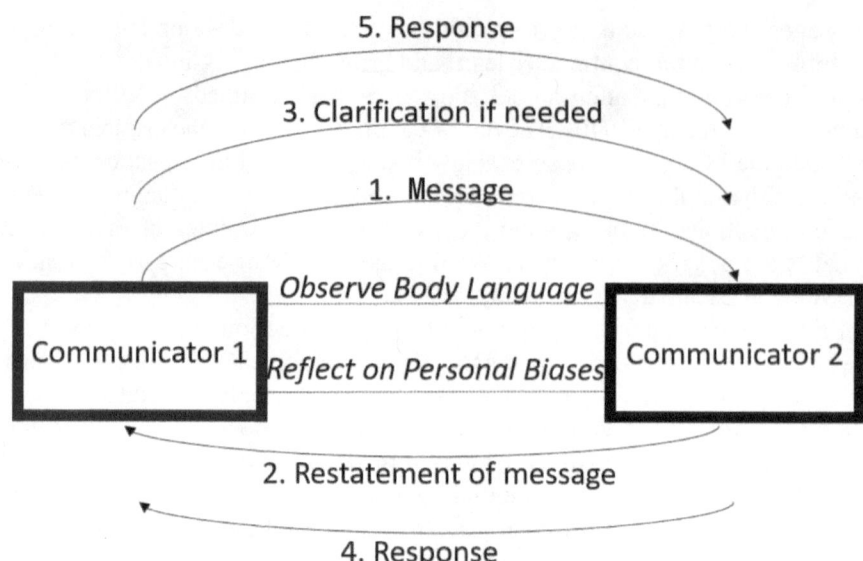
Figure 1.2. Education Communication Model

any type of communication, but specifically when difficult conversations or misunderstandings occur.

The Education Communication Model is a cyclical and iterative process that continues until an end is reached either through discussion or compromise. The italicized words in the middle are thought processes that each communicator needs to engage in before, during, and after the encounter.

WHAT IS EFFECTIVE COMMUNICATION?

While the strategies of communication are important, it is also important to strive for effective communication. "Effective communication is about more than just exchanging information. It's about understanding the emotion and intentions behind the information. As well as being able to clearly convey a message, you need to listen in a way that gains the full meaning of what's being said" (www.helpguide.org, 2018). How you communicate can positively or negatively impact the relationships in your professional life; therefore, effective strategies are important.

There are three basic principles to effective communication:

1. Ensure that spoken and written words, when combined, make grammatical sense so that messages are not misinterpreted and/or receiver bias does not interfere with the intended message.

Example:

Bad Grammar	Good Grammar
"I is going to go to the office."	"I am going to the office."
"They're house is in the woods."	"Their house is in the woods."

2. Ensure that nonverbal cues (tone of voice, eye contact, body language, hand gestures, emotional state) are delivered in a way that cannot be misinterpreted.

   A well-known UCLA study found that only around 7 percent of the meaning of spoken communication came from words alone, 55 percent came from facial expression (body language), and 38 percent came from the way the words were said (tone of voice).

3. Ensure that the environment and situation where the message is being delivered is appropriate.

   Examples include making sure that the environment where the conversation is occurring is safe, that there is not an "audience" (students) during important conversations between adults, or that everyone has had time to reflect and calm down if emotions are running high.

Overall, the questions that can be asked to determine the degree of effective communication are (Australian Institute of Business, 2018):

- How well do I/you work with others?
- Am I/are you able to take many different aspects and understand many different views?
- Am I/are you a team player who can help a team in achieving a common goal or solution to a problem?

IMPORTANT COMMUNICATION STRATEGIES

Communication strategies are the "blueprints for how information will be (or are) exchanged" (www.study.com, 2003–2018). As already stated, communication strategies include:

1. Verbal (written and oral)
2. Nonverbal (visual cues: physical distance, tone of voice, body language, clothing, tattoos, etc.)
3. Visual (websites, signs)

It is also believed that "55% of communication is body language, 38% is the tone of voice, and 7% is the actual words spoken" (Thompson, 2011). Additionally, when communicating through all or some of these types of communication strategies it is important that everything "matches." Your tone of voice and words match. Your physical distance and body language match. Your facial expressions and message match. It is important to convey the same message with all the strategies, so the receiver ensures they are receiving the intended message.

However, as already stated, some nonverbal communication strategies may not match due to the receiver's perceived biases, such as the sender's tattoos, accent, or piercings. As the receiver you need to be aware of your own biases, and as the sender you need to be aware of common biases "against" you.

While those three strategies are important, they are also quite general. The Public Relations Society of America (2018) outlined the Seven Cs of overcoming communication barriers, which is a way to reflect on communication strategies. The Seven Cs of communication are: Clarity, Credibility, Content, Context, Continuity, Capability, and Channels.

1. Are you clear in your communication style?
2. Are you a credible person and do you use credible information to support your communication?
3. Is the content relevant?
4. Is the context of the information focused on the common goal?
5. Are you continuous with the message you are portraying?
6. Are you capable of relaying the message effectively and are you capable of following through? Additionally, are you capable of working with many different types of people on many different problems?
7. Are you using the correct channels for the receiver?

The Seven Cs are important to consider in many professional fields. However, in the field of education, educators may also use a strategy known as the WOO factor—Winning Over Others. This is accomplished through eye contact, getting to know people, and finding commonalities. The strategies within the WOO factor will be discussed in our toolkit chapters.

Additionally, the field of business has outlined strategies that are important when communicating. They include developing a standardized way to communicate that includes details of how information will be dispersed and ensuring that enough information is provided for all to understand. This can be used in the field of education in multiple capacities, such as agendas for meetings, engaging in "I" statements, or beginning each team meeting with a get-to-know-you game.

In the education field, it is important that all communication with families and coworkers is honest and follows a structured "open door policy." The idea of being reachable, at defined times (in order to have a good work–life balance), is important. You, as an educator, can be reachable and reach families through different types of communication strategies, including:

1. Written (e.g., email or text) and oral (e.g., phone or face to face);
2. Body language during conversations or proximity to the person receiving the information;
3. Newsletters, websites, and clothing.

INTERPERSONAL SKILLS

Associated with the idea of effective communication is the concept of interpersonal skills. Specifically, effective communication is a key interpersonal skill, which is also known as people skills or employability skills. Can you relate to other people? Can you interact with other people? Interpersonal skills also correspond with the idea of emotional intelligence, which is the ability to sense and develop interpersonal skills, or the skills between people.

Interpersonal skills are essential in the education field because of the need to interact with a variety of people with a variety of backgrounds and personalities. There are over fifty interpersonal skills that are sought after in the business profession. These fifty skills can be a basis for key interpersonal skills in the education field. From that list, here are a few interpersonal skills that are needed in the field of education (Doyle, 2018):

- Active listening
- Behavioral skills ("good character")
- Caring and/or comforting and/or empathy
- Collaboration
- Communication
- Developing rapport (with students, coworkers, and families)
- Leadership
- Motivation
- Patience
- Problem-solving
- Responsibility
- Teamwork
- Tolerance
- Verbal communication

WHY IS COMMUNICATION IMPORTANT?

Communication is important to develop relationships, convey messages, and achieve common goals. Communicating is also vital to human life. *Forbes* contributor Greg Satell (2015) defends the idea that communication is today's most important skill. In summary, he states that communication is needed in every profession, it is bidirectional, and it goes hand in hand with knowledge. In order to transmit and receive knowledge, communication is essential.

Additionally, communication helps people express ideas and feelings and understand the thoughts and emotions of others (Speak, 2014). The president of New School University in New York, Bob Kerrey, stated that "people (who are) unable to express themselves clearly in writing limit their opportunities for professional salaried employment" (The College Board, 2004). All types of communication are important.

In other professions, such as business, communication is seen as a problem-solving activity. This is a mentality, a mentality of problem-solving, which can also be the focus of effective communication in the field of education. A problem is seen or identified and then can be solved or addressed through communication. Based on the knowledge available from business, communication helps identify the situation or problem, identify the next steps or action steps, and helps the involved parties decide on the best way to convey a solution to the problem. This is very similar to the practice of observing teachers, debriefing, and coming up with next steps toward a goal. An example of a structured, goal-centered agenda is in Figure 1.3.

Specifically, in the field of education, communication is important for:

- Students to understand concepts;
- Families to understand what is happening in schools;
- Community members/taxpayers to know how monies are being spent;
- Coworkers (educators) to understand common goals, curricular changes, and implementation practices.

A readily available example is the communication that was and still is needed around the implementation of the Common Core Standards in many states across the country. Having clear communication to teachers on how to implement, to principals on how to support staff, and to families on how the curricular changes will positively impact the education and growth of students was and still is essential. Since the rollout and implementation of the Common Core Standards in many states, media, social networks, families,

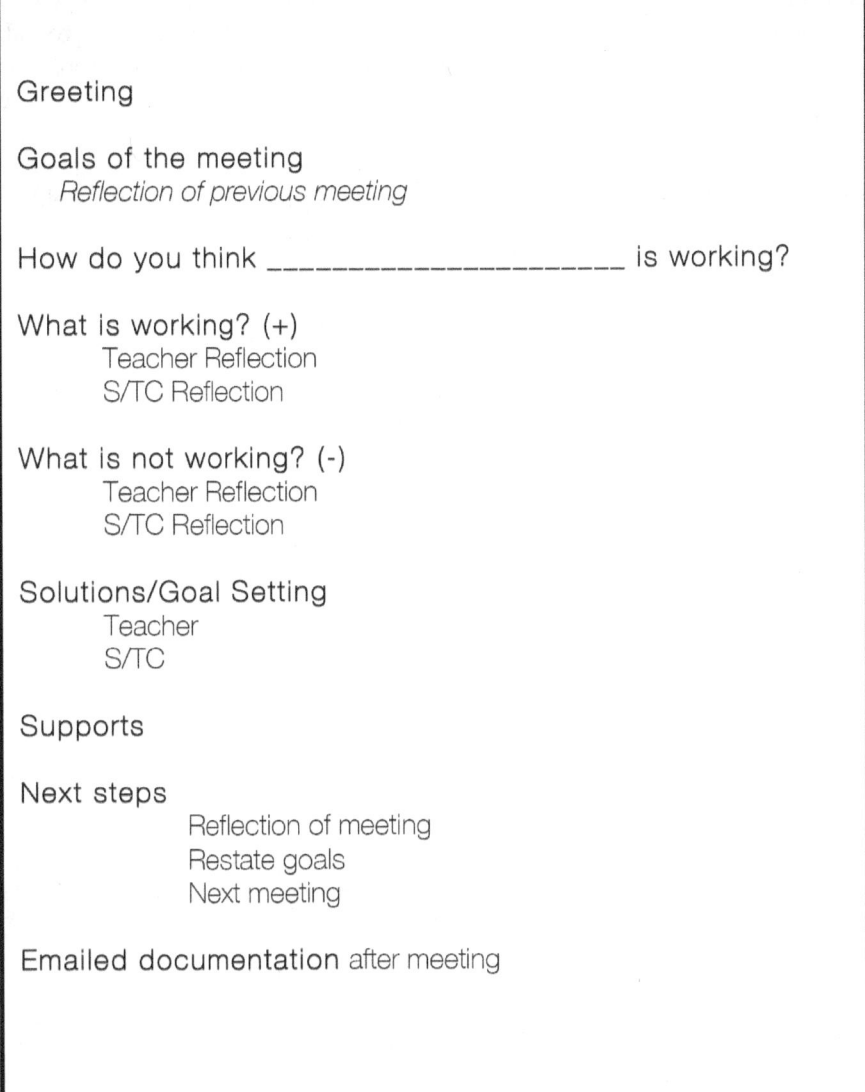

Figure 1.3. Structured Debrief Agenda

students, and educators have been the senders of communication as well as the receivers of communication.

Some of the information is positive, while other information is negative or critical. Regardless of the positive or negative nature of the communication, everyone is communicating and trying to get information across. However, it is important to keep the concepts of motivation, attitude, beliefs, background, values, and other ideas at the forefront during the communication of topics as controversial and wide-reaching as the implementation of the Common Core Standards.

Finally, as stated earlier in this chapter, it is important that we keep an open mind. The ability and willingness to reflect on key areas within the field of education is foundational. And one of those key areas is communication.

Chapter 2

Technology Communication

> *It is not about the technology; it's about sharing knowledge and information, communicating efficiently, building learning communities and creating a culture of professionalism in schools. These are the key responsibilities of all educational leaders.*
>
> —Marion Ginapolis (2011)

There are many aspects to consider when discussing communication. However, we have not yet discussed the most recent addition to the communication system: technology. In many cases technology rules our lives: our calendars are logged through technology, our verbal and written communication often occur through technology, and schools have had to design policies around the use of technology, specifically phone use, for both teachers and students.

Technology, especially since the invention and explosion of smartphones, has changed our communication styles and strategies. However, arguably, etiquette and the process of understanding how to appropriately and effectively use technology to communicate are still in the infancy stage.

As social beings who are getting used to the idea of being social via technology, it is difficult to understand the idea that technology is a one-way communication style, while most other styles of communication are two-way. The result? Individuals attempt to take two-way strategies and implement them into the one-way communication style, often leading to confusion, misinterpretations, and a breakdown of communication between two or more individuals.

There are a multitude of avenues to communication using only technology. Some of these avenues include, but are not limited to, emails, conference calls, web calls, web pages, text messages, Facebook pages, webinars, Twitter, and many other sites. When adding the next level of communicating via technology, there are more concepts to consider. However, while we will discuss some of the concepts, it is important to note that research is still being conducted to understand the impact and use of technology communication. It is also important to note that the field of education is arguably a field of customer service and relationships; therefore, communication outside of technology is still important in the field of education.

When communicating using technology, it is important to try to see the communication from different perspectives. Sometimes others can read and perceive information differently from the intended meaning because body language and tone of voice are left out of the equation.

Additionally, since messages using technology can be conveyed using a variety of images such as emojis, memes, text (long- and shorthand), gifs, pictures, and so on, it is important to be as clear as possible when having technology-based communication. Regardless of the image, the message and conveyed meaning depend on the receiver's attitude, frame of mind at the time of reading the communication, and other outside factors.

Here are two helpful tips when using technology to communicate:

1. If you are writing a sensitive message or responding to a difficult conversation, have a trusted peer read the message before sending to ensure that the message you intend to convey is the message that is being conveyed.
2. Do not respond immediately if the topic is sensitive or elicits a personal emotional feeling. As the creation of technology has created a society of immediacy, it is important to take time to reflect and think about responses before saying or sending something you might regret.

Specific to email communication:

1. Strong and informative subject line.
2. Proper punctuation.
3. Limit the number of jokes. (These are hard to convey without body language and tone.)
4. Proofread!

Finally, as discussed in the "Effective Communication" section, understanding the emotions and intentions behind the information conveyed is also part of the communication cycle. However, emotions are hard to convey via digital formats. Therefore, it is important that everything is not communicated in a digital format. Having verbal—preferably face-to-face—conversation is still an important aspect of communication, even in the technological age.

Technology Communication

The way technology is used as a communication device and how it is constantly changing adds more obstacles and key points when discussing communication with others. Using technology, people can have entire conversations only using emojis or memes. Figure 2.1 displays an example of this type of communication.

From the example below, it may be hard for some to come away with the same meaning.

Meaning 1: "I voted today. It felt great. Hallelujah."
"I see. Hmm, well I went dancing and then to play with cats."
"You are crazy. Do you want to go get food? I want to go to yoga first, but then we can go. It is supposed to rain so bring your umbrella."
"Cool. Thanks for the invitation but I am tired. I am going to bed."
"What? Go get food with me and then go to bed."
"I played football video games, drank, listened to music, watched TV, went to the bathroom, and now it's time for bed."
"Fine. That is disappointing. Good night."

Figure 2.1. Emoji Conversation

Meaning 2: "I checked in at the American Gym to lift weights. It was nice. People were working out and giving high fives."
"I went looking for dancing but couldn't find any, so I went home to hang out with my cat."
"Funny. I am hungry. Do you want pizza, fries, or soup?"
"Nothing, I am tired. Thanks though. It's my bedtime."
"Wow. Okay. Well, I am going to go get pizza, fries, and soup, then go to bed. I will see you later."
"I played video games, threw around a football, drank while I listened to music on the TV, and now I am getting ready for bed."
"Hugs. I am tired too."

While entire conversations can be completed through images, written messages can also be delivered in direct, short, and arguably fewer personal ways, such as text messages or instant messages. Many companies are installing instant messenger–like programs or encouraging workers to engage with each other through social network sites such as Facebook Messenger, Gchat (Gmail chat), or Google Hangouts in order to accomplish tasks.

Specifically, media companies and companies with freelance employees or people living all over the world are beginning to use internal communication (messaging) tools to increase collaboration and productivity. Companies have found that after integrating internal messaging tools, people are able to connect more and create a workplace with more transparency and collaboration. This allows everyone to contribute and be recognized for their contribution.

Technology, specifically social media, is also changing the way educators communicate and form professional learning communities (PLCs). Research specifically on the impact of social media on the profession of education is outlined in chapter 10.

While technology has many benefits, the idea of change and generational gaps of technological knowledge can impact the implementation of technology in many areas, including education.

As a professor I know that some of my students use technology in a different way than I do. Specifically, it is so difficult for me and other professors to understand the disengagement of students and their email. Anecdotally we have found that college-age students do not check their email as much as people in their later twenties and above. However, communicating through Snapchat and text messaging is engaged in more often. One work-around we have found in our program is to use the app GroupMe, which comes across essentially as a group text message.

Regardless of how you or the people you communicate with use technology, it is imperative to remember that tailoring communication to the "receiver" will decrease highly negative emotional responses. It is all about perception. If you are attempting to communicate with a staff member or parent who dislikes talking on the phone but prefers to text, then text to communicate with the individual. Personally, I know this to be true. I do not like to talk on the phone, so when I introduce my syllabus each semester, I inform the students of my preferences for communicating with me, and I respect their preferred communication style in return.

Interestingly, though, the concepts of texting and types of technology communication are becoming robot-like. When you are texting, your device provides you with words that you may be typing, giving you things to write. Arguably, we are becoming robot-like in our communication due to technology. Regardless, it is important to communicate honestly, truthfully, and most importantly, respectfully if using technology to communicate.

BRAIN DEVELOPMENT AND TECHNOLOGY

The reliance on technology and communicating using technology also impacts how our brains work and the development of our brains. Since technology being used in a wider context in society is still in its infancy, research is limited. However, there are initial findings on the way the brain is changing as technology increases in our lives.

Current research shows that technology can be both beneficial and harmful for technology/digital natives, which are students that are "native speakers" of the digital language (computers, videos, video games, social media, and so forth). As all educators know, the brain is very malleable, especially for young students. Therefore, engaging with technology changes the wiring in the brain, which has both costs and benefits.

Some of the perceived costs include decreased attention spans and the way in which humans pay attention to information being presented. Conversely, benefits include the expansion of knowledge by having constant engagement and by asking and discovering new things using Google searches.

Overall, the knowledge gained from the world of business and research focused on educators is reporting that the new and engaging ways to interact with each other via technology other are changing communication between and among groups, both personally and professionally.

TECHNOLOGY AND FAMILY COMMUNICATION

While there is one whole toolkit in this book focused on family communication, in this chapter it is important to discuss the impact of technology. During an #edchat radio segment, using technology tools to communicate with families was the main talking point. Interestingly, one of the areas of discussion focused on communicating "too much" with families using technology. Does technology make communication impersonal or too overwhelming? The participants were split, but it is a great question for educators to ask themselves in the age of technology.

Furthermore, technology can create an environment where teachers think, "Well, parents have access to everything online, so why don't they know their student's grade?" Having the grades online does provide access, but not every parent checks the technology resources. Therefore teachers need to ensure that focused communication does happen and not just assume it occurs. Essentially, teachers need to ask themselves, Is the method of communication or the message that is communicated more important? The ability to communicate asynchronously is convenient, but has the practice of oversharing become common?

Chapter 3

Communication Barriers and Blocks

> *Effective communication requires messages to be conveyed clearly between communicators, but along the way there are many communication barriers that can create misunderstandings and misinterpretations of your message.*
>
> —Communication Studies (2019)

Communication barriers and blocks stop conversations, regardless of the communication method. Therefore, blocks and barriers are essential to learn about and recognize in order to improve staff morale, community and school relationships, as well as family-to-school relationships. While both barriers and blocks have the same wider definition (stopping communication), they also have specific examples that differ, and therefore they are used in different aspects of society.

For example, barriers are discussed in the business and medical fields, while blocks are generally discussed when talking about parenting. Both blocks and barriers are essential to know as educators because of the wide range of individuals we interact with daily. When interacting with students, understanding communication blocks is important. When interacting with colleagues or families, communication barriers are important to understand.

COMMUNICATION BARRIERS

While barriers generally are used in the medical and business fields, as stated above, they can also impact the field of education. The five key barriers are:

1. Language
2. Cultural Diversity

3. Gender Differences
4. Status Differences
5. Physical Separation

These barriers can create challenges when aiming for effective communication, relationship building, and reaching shared goals. Specifically, when there is a language barrier it is difficult to fully explain expectations and provide feedback. Language barriers may include the inability to speak the same language or difficulty conveying a message in a shared language. Additionally, they could include the inability of the receiver to understand an unfamiliar accent, even if the language is the same (e.g., northern and southern United States accents).

Language barriers in education can occur between multiple parties. How can you communicate the progress of a student or concern to a family member if there is a language barrier? Educators can learn from the field of business and ensure that a translator is always present when communicating. Also, make sure to translate documents using a native speaker (not Google Translate), use both telling and showing methods (visuals), and, if needed, use repetition.

Language barriers can also occur if there is specific professionally related jargon or language that outsiders to the profession do not understand. When overcomplicated or technical terms are used without context, a language barrier between receiver and sender can also occur. Therefore, it is important to use words that are not based in the professional jargon and allow for questions to clarify any misunderstandings.

Cultural diversity barriers are grounded in the definition of cultural diversity: "the existence of a variety of cultural or ethnic groups within a society." The diversity of cultures around the world and within your community or school building creates an environment of potential barriers. Cultures provide people with ways of thinking—ways of seeing, hearing, and interpreting the world. Therefore, perceptions are skewed or can differ between and among individuals with different cultural backgrounds. Cultures determine the meanings of words and views of the world, and they can increase misunderstandings.

For example, a native speaker of Spanish who is from Spain may have a different meaning for a word than a Spanish-speaking Mexican. If a translator uses Spain Spanish for a Mexican Spanish speaker, a completely different meaning may be conveyed.

Stella Ting-Toomey, a professor of human communication studies at California State University, Fullerton, describes three ways cultural diversity can create a barrier to communication. First is the idea of cognitive constraints, or the frames of references individuals have depending on their background and culture.

Second is the idea of behavior constraints, or the behaviors that are acceptable or not acceptable in specific cultures. For example, eye contact and personal space convey various messages depending on the culture.

Finally, there is the idea of emotional constraint, or the differing ways cultures display emotions. In some cultures, it is okay to show emotion and be vocal about a felt emotion, while in other cultures it is not okay to show emotion because showing emotion is seen as a weakness.

Gender difference barriers can impact communication. Gender differences can be based on gender stereotypes or identified traits that differ between genders. In Table 3.1 is a visual representation of gender difference barriers based on stereotypes and researched traits (Meier, 2018).

The differences in gender communication can create a barrier because men expect everyone to communicate as they do, and women expect everyone to communicate as they do. When the other gender does not fall into the expected communication style, barriers (and sometimes frustrations) occur.

While it is not always politically correct or socially acceptable to talk about the differences between genders, there are scientific findings that show men and women's brains are different. "The right and left hemispheres of the male and female brains are not set up the same way. For instance, females tend to

Table 3.1. Women versus Men: Gender Differences

Stereotype/Traits	Women	Men
Emotional vs. Factual	Focus more on feelings, senses, meanings, and talk about people. Communicate to gain insights by asking questions.	Focus more on facts and logic. Talk about tangible things (e.g., sports, food, drinks). Communicate to give information, facts, and logic.
Motivations	Try to learn about new people and gain trust.	Try to establish credibility by talking about achievements and responsibilities.
Misunderstandings	Report that men do not take them seriously or treat them as professionals because of the focus on relationship building. Report that men are aggressive because of their focus on achievements.	Report that women may interpret what they say in an unintended way, so they do not know how to approach a topic with women.
Conflicts	Conflicts have long-lasting effects.	Move on quickly from conflicts.
Problem-solving	Talk to other women when a problem or conflict arises.	Deal with conflicts or issues internally.

have verbal centers on both sides of the brain, while males tend to have verbal centers on only the left hemisphere. This is a significant difference" (Jantz, 2014). While these differences of brain use do not point to "good" or "bad," it is important to consider how female and male brains differ in order to see conversations from multiple sides and/or become aware of how gender can influence communication.

Specifically, in the field of education most teachers are female, and most administrators are male. Therefore, it is important to understand how leaders can communicate effectively with their staff and how staff can effectively communicate with coworkers with the common knowledge of brain differences.

This is also an important concept to remember when working and communicating with students of different genders. Girls will more likely be influenced by talking and feelings, while boys will be more influenced by facts and action. Again, while we do not want to point out gender differences, it is important to understand that there are scientific, biological differences between most boys' and girls' brains, as outlined by scientific research.

Status difference barriers can also impact effective communication. Specifically, status differences relate to the hierarchy of an organization. In some organizations the status of an individual is of utmost importance. This would be a high-context culture. Essentially, everyone is not seen as equal.

In other organizations the status of an individual does not impact communication because everyone is seen as an equal, from the maintenance worker to the CEO or superintendent. This is a low-context culture. Interacting in an environment where status matters and everyone is seen as having a hierarchal place can decrease staff morale and motivation, thus creating a barrier to communication between different "levels" of the hierarchy.

Physical separation barriers are "the environmental and natural conditions that act as a barrier in communication in sending message(s) from sender to receiver" (Businesstopia, 2018). Some examples of physical separation barriers include interior workplace design (i.e., walls), technological problems (i.e., lack of Internet), and noise. Overall, physical barriers can create situations where communication is cut off (phone connection), not heard fully (noisy background), or misunderstood.

There are various reasons why physical barriers can impact communication. Distortion is one cause. When the process of encoding and decoding the message is impacted, mainly due to human perceptions or distractions, a barrier is created. Noise is another factor in physical barriers to communication. When an environment is noisy, messages can be perceived in unclear ways.

Sometimes, for hearing people, this is a result of trying to "listen" through lip-reading during a noisy concert or in a chaotic classroom environment.

Furthermore, noise barriers are also referred to in cases of illegible handwriting or inaccurate typing, thus creating a message that is not fully conveyed or could be misunderstood.

The outside factors of environment and weather of a specific area can also be a physical barrier. Thunder, rain, and wind all can impact the message being conveyed. Additionally, temperatures inside or outside can also impact messages. If someone is too hot or too cold, it is often hard to pay attention.

Internal environmental factors also are guided by personal thoughts preventing full attention to the situation and message. It has been found that for every eight minutes, humans only fully pay attention to four minutes, potentially missing important information. This is due to distractions and the increasingly fast-paced society.

Time and distance are physical barriers, specifically when working with people in time zones that differ from your own. Along with distance is the understanding that a decision needs to be agreed upon as to what technology will be used in order to communicate. If face-to-face communication is not available through video conferencing, communicating through voice only can also be a barrier because the parties communicating cannot see any body language, which adds to the understanding of the communication.

Finally, another physical barrier is the idea of information overflow. In the technologically advanced world of today, with constant information at our fingertips, being overloaded with information can create a barrier to effective communication. If an email is "too long" for the receiver to read or the important information is not highlighted, the message and the desired outcome will be unlikely to occur. Along with this idea of information overload is the concept of lack of interest or irrelevance to the receiver.

Overall, barriers impact the world of business and medicine but have the potential to impact the field of education as well. Each of the key barriers influences the classroom and school environment, specifically diversity, language, and gender.

COMMUNICATION BLOCKS

The concept of communication blocks is generally associated with parenting. Many professionals refer to communication blocks when discussing parents' interactions with adolescents and teenagers. However, the idea of communication blocks can also be used in the field of education. Therefore, understanding the blocks that can stop communication abruptly between parties is important knowledge to have and to begin to recognize within ourselves.

There are two definitions of communication blocks:

1. "Any remark or attitude on the part of the listener that injures the speaker's self-esteem to the extent that communication is broken off" (Klein, 2013).
2. "Any words, tone of voice, or body language that influence a person sharing a problem" (Popkin, 2014) result in the end of collaborative communication.

Many times, communication blocks overlap or are synonymous with the idea of coping strategies. When a conversation occurs, specifically one with a problem to solve, everyone has a way to cope with that situation as the receiver; some might say it is our innate reaction to difficult conversations. Therefore, being able to recognize personal communication blocks and communication blocks in others can create effective and meaningful communication that is constant rather than stopped.

Everyone has coping communication blocks that may not be readily acknowledged; however, they do infiltrate communication. These communication blocks, as outlined in the book *Active Parenting* by Michael Popkin, PhD, Gordon Training International, and with additions from my own professional career as an educator, include:

1. Commanding (Popkin and Gordon Training)
2. Giving Advice (Popkin and Gordon Training)
3. Placating (Popkin)
4. Interrogating (Popkin and Gordon Training)
5. Distracting (Popkin and Gordon Training)
6. Psychologizing or Analyzing (Popkin and Gordon Training)
7. Sarcasm or Ridiculing (Popkin and Gordon Training)
8. Moralizing (Popkin and Gordon Training)
9. Know-It-All (Popkin)
10. Threatening (Gordon Training)
11. Lecturing with Logic (Gordon Training)
12. Judging or Criticizing (Gordon Training)
13. Praising or Agreeing (Gordon Training)
14. Name-Calling or Ridiculing (Gordon Training)
15. Sympathizing and Supporting (Gordon Training)
16. Ignoring or Ghosting (Reinking)
17. Negative Emotional Response (Reinking)
18. Gaslighting (Reinking)

Each of these communication blocks impacts the reciprocal communication relationship between parities. Again, while these communication blocks are based in parenting techniques, they will be described for use in the field of education. Additionally, it is important to note that personalities can impact the perception of these communication blocks; however, these are general ideas to understand when discussing communication blocks.

Commanding is when a quick solution is provided. It is also referred to as ordering or directing. When messages are received as commanding, the receiver does not feel as if their feelings or needs are important. Additionally, the commanding communication block creates a relationship where the receiver does not feel accepted, resulting in a feeling of resentment, anger, and hostility. An example with a student could be "Stop fidgeting around," instead of "Thomas, I see that you need to move around a little bit. Would you like to stand by your desk during this lesson?"

The communication block of giving advice, while well intentioned, sends the message that one of the parties in the situation does not have confidence in the other individual's judgment. Situations where providing advice or solutions is the go-to communication block create conditions in which the receiver, in most cases a child, might become resentful or too dependent on the person giving advice. An example is "I am the teacher and I know what is best, so do not sit by your friend," instead of posing a reflective question such as "Do you think it may help you learn if you sit by your friend or sit somewhere else during work time? Why do you think that? Let us think back to other parts of our day."

Placating is also known as pacifying or trying to make someone less angry at a situation. This is the block some people use when they have the desire to help someone feel better. An example is "Everything will be okay. Here, the piece of candy you want (so you stop crying)." The opposite, or more productive response could be "I hear that you are sad through your words. I can see that you are crying and may want something. I am here to listen and help you cope (without candy)."

Interrogating, as a communication block, includes the action of constantly questioning the individual, which displays suspicion or doubt. At times, when individuals are being questioned, they can feel threatened by not understanding why the questioning is occurring, or they can feel defensive, which derails the communication. Overall, interrogating severely limits the freedom of the receiver (child or student).

An example is "Did you put your homework in your desk like I told you to? Are you sure? Where is your homework?" Conversely, a more positive statement may be "Where do we put our homework when we get in the classroom? Thank you for following directions."

Distracting, which is also referred to as withdrawing, humoring, or diverting, is the act of communicating to the individual that you are not interested in what they have to say and do not respect their feelings. For example, if a child or student approaches an adult with serious intent, focused on their emotions, but is responded to with humor, the child feels rejected and/or hurt. Therefore, that communication avenue is now damaged and blocked.

It is important as the adult in the life of a child, or an adult communicating with another adult, to validate the feeling the sender is communicating and not divert the conversation to something else. For example, "Oh, she told you she did not want to be friends anymore? Well, I guess you will just have to find another crazy girl to hang out with." Addressing the emotion and not making a joke or diverting the conversation may sound like "She does not want to be your friend anymore? That must be very sad." Remember, you do not have to solve everything.

Psychologizing, analyzing, or diagnosing is a communication block that communicates to the receiver that you have figured out the issue by psychoanalyzing the individual and can expose the issue, creating resentment and embarrassment. Examples of this would be sentences that begin with, "I know why" or "I can see through you." Rather than making psychologizing statements, eradicating a communication block in this situation could include a statement such as "I am here to listen. I can see that you are angry." Part of this, as with most communication blocks, is recognizing the emotion and just "sitting in it." Emotions are okay to have.

Sarcasm and ridiculing, in general and as a communication block, can have devastating effects on the self-image and self-esteem of a student. Sarcasm, ridiculing, and name-calling create a relationship where the receiver is less likely to change but rather will focus on the negative message. If the message is heard often enough, it can become internalized.

An example of a parent or teacher responding with sarcasm would be "You are ridiculous. I guess it's just the end of the world, isn't it?" A more positive and encouraging statement could be "I can see that you are very sad that it happened. I would be sad also." Real-life situations include a boss tearing up a piece of work in front of the rest of the staff while asking the rhetorical question "Are you an idiot? That is not how it is done."

The communication block of moralizing or preaching occurs when the words "should," "ought," or "must" are incorporated into the response. Those specific words can cause guilt or mistrust. Examples include "You shouldn't feel that way" or "You should just walk right up to that bully and tell him to stop." A more positive and encouraging statement could be "What I hear you saying is that it hurts when they say those words to you. That is bullying, and it is hurtful. Would you like to talk about solutions together?"

Know-it-all is when a parent, teacher, or colleague conveys the message that they know everything and you do not. This suggest that you are lacking knowledge that is "quite simple." For example, "You seriously did not know how to turn the copy machine on? That is so easy. Look, it's right here." Instead of putting down a person, a more positive response could be "I can help you. The 'on' button is right here. It took me a little bit to figure it out also."

Threatening or warning is another communication block that sends a message to the receiver of their apparent submissiveness and inferiority. The receiver views this type of communication block as disrespectful. Many times, what is communicated are warnings or threats if something does not occur or is not accomplished. This communication block happens between adults and children or between two adults. An example is "If you do not turn in your lesson plan on time, I will write you up," without a conversation or development of a firm foundational relationship. Conversely, a more positive communication interaction could be "The due date for the lesson plans is Friday. Please let me know if there is anything I can do to help you meet our goal."

Lecturing with logical arguments is a way of communicating by showing the facts and logic behind a situation. This is a block because people often do not like to be bluntly shown or told they are wrong. This could take the form of a lecture of facts or an email with logical reasons why something "should" be completed. Many times, this creates resentment. An example is "If you hadn't waited until the last minute to plan your lesson, maybe you would have been more prepared." While the statement may be true, pointing it out will only create resentment. A different response could be "I can see that it was turned in late. Is there a way we can work together in order to meet deadlines? I would really like to help you be successful on our team."

Judging or criticizing is also known as disagreeing or blaming. This is a communication block that messages negative criticism to a receiver based on evaluations. It is hard to find someone who innately enjoys being judged. Therefore, this common communication block of judging creates a negative self-concept for the receiver. Additionally, when a receiver (child, student, or coworker) hears negative criticisms enough, a self-fulfilling prophecy begins to take shape.

For example, if a person is told they are lazy day in and day out, they will internalize the idea of being lazy and display that attribute to live up to the expectations of those around them. However, you can "fill their bucket" with many positive things, and this self-fulfilling prophecy will become reality also.

The communication block of praising or agreeing may be controversial. Many people argue that praise is good for motivation and self-esteem. However, praise can also have negative effects. Many times, praise can be interpreted as manipulative, no matter how well intended. Others may feel embarrassed or uncomfortable with praise. Still others may have received praise for so much of their life that they rely on it and when it, is not given, the person's self-worth is diminished.

As an educator myself, I have heard these sentiments frequently. Therefore, in the field of education, it is important to reflect and question the use of praise in classroom settings and with coworkers.

The communication style or block of sympathizing and supporting is not as helpful as most people want to believe. Many times, people support or console because from a young age people are taught in many cultures to console a person displaying emotions. However, sympathizing can be seen by a receiver (child or coworker) as the sender trying to change them, which in turn stops communication. An example is "Don't feel bad. It will all be alright. Just feel better," while rubbing the receiver's arm or hugging them. While this is an instinct for some people, it can also be a communication block. Instead of telling the person what to feel or do, along with touch, just be in the moment with them. "I hear you stating that you are embarrassed. Would you like to talk about it?" Secondly, if you are going to touch someone, please make sure they are okay with touch—not everyone is, and invading a personal bubble can put up guards that create blocks.

The term "ghosting" is a common phrase in the dating world; however, it can occur in any relationship. Ghosting is defined as "ending a personal relationship with someone by suddenly and without explanation withdrawing from all communication" (dictionary.com). This can occur as a block when a colleague or parent completely ignores emails, phone calls, or conversations.

While it is usually defined as a strategy used in a personal relationship, the concept of ignoring or ghosting in the field of education, or any other professional field, is also prominent. If you are the one ghosting, please be aware of this behavior. If you are the one being ghosted, recognize that it is a block and that addressing the situation head-on, with respect, may be the best strategy.

Negative emotional responses can impact communication and relationships. Negative emotional responses, as we will discuss in our toolkits, are defined by the receiver's perception. However, perceptions can be deceiving at times. Regardless, if the receiver's perception is that the emotional response of the sender is negative, such as yelling, crying, or becoming physically or verbally aggressive, this can then create a communication block.

Most educators can tell stories of experiences when students' family members have become verbally aggressive, which ultimately results in negative emotional responses and sometimes diminished positive relationships. For example, an educator reflected that a police officer was required to stand outside the classroom during meetings with a specific family. This restricted the meeting times and days.

Finally, the concept of gaslighting is not always associated with communication blocks, but the act of gaslighting someone will block communication in the future. "Gaslighting is a tactic in which a person or entity, in order to gain more power, makes a victim question their reality" (Sarkis, 2017). This can occur between individuals who have opposite personality traits, such as an authoritarian and a permissive personality type.

Gaslighting is a strategy used to control a situation or person. This can be used by a parent to control how their student is treated in school, by an administrator who controls how curriculum is taught, or by a colleague who "runs" the school. Addressing situations through gaslighting creates animosity and blocks communication. Some signs of gaslighting include compulsive lying, denying that statements or actions were made (even if there is proof), aligning people against you, and generally manipulating a situation and the individuals around the situation.

As is evident in the numerous descriptions of communication blocks and barriers, the receiver often feels subordinate or inferior to the parent or colleague engaging in the communication block. This can damage relationships in classrooms, schools, and families. Being aware of personal communication barriers and blocks, as well as recognizing them in other people, is important when discussing communication and creates a foundational understanding for all readers as we move through this book.

What is important to remember, however, is that even if the communication block or barrier is recognized and communication is cooperative, not every situation will be "solved."

Reflection Questions:

- What communication blocks do you use in the workplace and at home with various people?
- What communication blocks do you recognize in coworkers?
- What questions are still circling in your head?

Chapter 4

Difficult Conversations

Feeling uncomfortable during a difficult conversation is common; embracing the discomfort and moving past it is more challenging.

—Kimberly Datchuk (2018)

Difficult conversations are conversations that may be more conflict based or argumentative (Stone, Patton, Heen, & Fisher, 2010). Other researchers, who focus on building positive leadership skills and strong workplaces, define difficult conversations as situations in which at least two parties are engaged and where

(a) there are differing opinions, perceptions, and needs/wants
(b) feelings and emotions run strong
(c) the consequences or stakes for us (participants) are significant. (Russell Consulting, 2009)

Common characteristics of difficult conversations include a lack of trust, limited active listening, a goal of "winning," and emotions running high, specifically the emotions of fear and anxiety (2009).

Although difficult conversations are inevitable, there are numerous professions around the world that rely on positive or effective communication skills. Specifically, in the field of education, school staff, including teachers, administrators, paraprofessionals, and administrative assistants, are some of those professionals who rely on customer service or professional communication to develop positive relationships with multiple stakeholders. Professional communication can take many forms, as discussed in previous chapters. However, it is essential to know how to participate in difficult conversations when they arise.

When thinking about communicating with various parties in the field of education, it is important to remember that while the receiver or audience is often blamed for not accepting the message, a lot depends on how the sender is perceiving the environment and the chosen channel or mode of communication. A lot of the communication control is in the hands of the sender. Therefore, it is important for the sender (predominantly educators and administrators in the field of education) to have a solid grasp on the concepts introduced in chapters 1–3 before moving on to the strategies for participating in difficult conversations.

Individuals in the field of education have experienced or will experience interactions with supervisors, coworkers, students, or family members where communication styles and conversation topics become difficult or uncomfortable for one or both of the parties involved. It is important to note here that both parties will not necessarily have the same reaction to a conversation or topic. Reactions to and perceptions of conversations rely heavily on personal backgrounds, emotional states, and other outside factors (Lightfoot, 2004).

For example, some family members (i.e., parents or guardians) might have experienced teachers in the past who labeled a student as "slow" or "bad" or who did not engage the student in a growth mindset. This can result in aggressive or combative communication from day one. Conversely, teachers may have years of experience or just one experience with families who did not listen to or value the teachers' professionalism and classroom goals. Therefore, teachers might unconsciously begin conversations with families based on preconceived notions from past experiences with other families.

Other dichotomous relationships can also occur in school environments. Teachers may have preconceived notions about their administrators or disagree with administrative choices. On the other hand, administrators may not fully understand the stress teachers feel in the classroom day in and day out. Regardless of the individual perceptions based on past experiences, this tense dichotomous relationship can lead to conversations that are difficult to start, have, and finish.

INSTINCTUAL REACTIONS AND EMOTIONS

Sixty-six percent of people who engage in or plan for a difficult conversation have the instinctive reaction to feel stressed or anxious, which is generally termed a "negative emotional response." Additionally, 57 percent of people report that they would do almost anything to avoid having a difficult conversation (Schneider, 2018; Stone, Patton, Heen, & Fisher, 2010). However, difficult conversations are inevitable.

The emotions of fear, anxiety, and other "negative" or stress-ridden reactions are a result of the brain taking over during the situation. The brain taking over is a deep-rooted instinct in the human body as a survival mechanism from eons past. This instinct engages natural reactions rather than thought-out reactions. When difficult conversation, or stressful conversations, are engaged in or planned for, instincts kick in. Some instinctual reactions include a racing heart rate, an increase in blood pressure, overreacting sweat glands, a feeling of butterflies in the stomach, fidgeting, and other fight-or-flight responses.

Why do our instincts take over? They take over because our brain is relying on the old or primitive brain, which includes the brain stem, medulla, pons, reticular formation, thalamus, cerebellum, amygdala, hypothalamus, and hippocampus. Specifically, the thalamus takes in the sensory input, which is then relayed to the amygdala. When the amygdala receives a message, the instinctual memory and instinctual self engage, which results in the individual's automatic reaction, including thoughtless emotional responses.

These thoughtless emotional responses are also known as instincts (fight or flight). Additionally, the hippocampus is the center of emotion, memory, and the autonomic nervous system. All of this impacts the instinctual reaction when engaging in or preparing for a difficult conversation.

While we like to imagine the emotions are set, current research suggests that emotions are malleable based on place and setting. Depending on where we are, emotions can change, and depending on our cultural context, emotions can change. If you get anxious in a school building that you went to as a child, but not in the school building your child attends, that shows that emotions in reference to situations are malleable. Interestingly, language and cultural contexts also impact emotion. All humans do not experience emotion in the same way primarily based on language.

For example, at funerals in America it is generally a time for sadness and grieving. However, in a tribe located in Ghana it is tradition for the children to play with the corpse of their grandparents and sometimes even hide the corpse as a practical joke. The emotions associated with an event are malleable and cultural. One more example is that in Tunisian there is no word meaning "sadness"; however, in Russia there are many types of sadness based on the words used in their language.

Regardless, when the old brain "takes over," based on genetics and language, it helps us make sense of the situation. We may feel threatened or disrespected. Maybe our profession is being questioned or a family member's child is being bullied. We may feel like we have lost control of the situation or are vulnerable. Maybe a family member of a student is yelling at us about their child and is not engaged in active listening, resulting in a lack of effective communication.

Our instincts may take over when we sense a communication block. Maybe we are being ghosted by a family member who does not want to hear about their child's behavior. Or maybe we are being commanded by an administrator to implement a new procedure that we do not fully agree with or understand. Regardless of the old brain's reaction, it is important to recognize our instincts. And if our reactions are not conducive to effective communication, we need to reflect on strategies that will transform our natural reactions. For example, if you become very anxious, taking time to engage in deep breaths and counting to ten is a tried-and-true de-escalation method.

While our instincts are deemed by society and culture as "normal" or "abnormal," it is also important to remember cultural barriers. Our society sets "norms" for reactions and emotions. However, these differ between countries, cultures, and even languages. For example, some people may cry when they are angry. People perceiving that person may think they are sad; however, the emotion of anger in one person may create tears, while in another person it may create numbness or yelling. While crying in response to anger is not a "normal" response in our culture, yelling is. From this example, individuals cannot guess or assume they know how someone is feeling based on looking at their face, words, or body language because personal "old brain" instincts take over.

Emotions are not in the face and body, and humans must make connections to provide meaning. Essentially our brains are making assumptions to determine an emotion that is expressed. We rely heavily on these assumptions because we are sometimes correct; however, we are not correct all the time, and this leads to misunderstandings and wrong assumptions.

Interestingly, though, some technology companies, such as Facebook and Google, are trying to design emotion detection systems. However, researchers in the field of emotions do not support this endeavor. If our own brains have a hard time making sense of others' emotions, it would be very difficult to teach a program the learned behaviors of humans.

For example, when individuals try to "read" a situation to determine the emotional status of someone else, we take into context all the surrounding events. Maybe someone is crying but they are crying after the birth of their healthy baby. Or we may see someone smiling, but we can tell they are sad and just "putting on a brave face" as their loved one goes in for exploratory surgery. Emotions need context, just as conversations need context to decode. So, communication is important, but it is also confusing when emotions and instincts take over.

Emotional responses are purely predictions our minds make about someone else or about the situation. However, some people assume that humans are prewired for specific emotions in response to specific situations. This is a common misconception that can cause dysfunctional communication and/or relationships.

For example, some cultures do not have the emotion of sadness, and other cultures have various words for the term "love." For someone who views the emotion of sadness (crying) as a normal emotion but interacts with someone from a culture that does not have the emotion of sadness, confusion can ensue.

It is important to remember that not all people are the same and emotions are not prewired; context and cultural knowledge are crucial. Therefore, it is difficult to know what someone is feeling or thinking by purely looking at one's perceived body language, words, or facial expressions in response to a situation, especially when engaging in difficult and emotional conversations. Overall, emotions are subjective. There is not one single objective measure for emotions.

For example, when some people are embarrassed or angry they cry. This can be perceived by others as sadness or something to comfort in another person; however, the action of crying does not always mean "I need comfort."

While it is hard to accurately perceive emotions in relation to communication, it is important to recognize that expressions of negative emotions can cause distress and hurt relationships. As a reminder, negative emotional responses are defined by the perception of the receiver. However, perceptions can be deceiving. Specific negative emotional responses depend on the situation but often include anger, sadness, greed, and animosity. Overall, emotional responses, both positive and negative, are critical to communication and relationship building in all types of contexts with the field of education and beyond.

Real-Life Scenario

"Ms. Crum, you need to come see me when the school day is over."
"Am I in trouble?"
"No, I just need to talk to you."
"Can you tell me what it is about?"
"No, I would rather do it in person."
By this point I had a sinking feeling in my stomach and my tears began. I had no idea what was going to happen, but I could sense a difficult conversation and my instinct was to cry and apologize over and over. Sensing my anxiety, my administrator said, "You are not in trouble, you have just missed a lot of work and I want to support you."

At this point my tears began. I was glad we were on the phone, but I knew that she could hear my quivering voice. "Okay, I am so sorry. I will make sure to come into your office. I am just so sorry."

Crying, embarrassment, all of that was and always is just my instinct. It is embarrassing that that is my reaction. It makes me feel weak. But it is an instinct and happens to many people in my family, and we just learn to cope with this reaction and embarrassment.

Reflection Questions:

- How might you feel in this situation? What would be your instincts?

Communication, especially when instinctual emotions are involved, is hard to decipher, but that is why practice, self-reflection, knowledge, and learning from other professions is so important.

LEARNING FROM HEALTHCARE

Difficult conversations do not occur only in education. However, there is very limited research and information available specifically for educators focused on difficult conversations. Therefore, relying on other professions, such as healthcare, to build a foundation for the field of education is imperative. The information gathered from these research studies is important to understand and use as a knowledge base when developing a toolkit for educators. Two studies will be briefly described.

First, Boston Children's Hospital developed a program focused on improving staff communication strategies with patients and families after noticing residences were having many tense conversations without focused training. It is called the Program to Enhance Relational and Communication Skills (PERCS). This program was launched to "help practitioners become more competent and prepared to engage in difficult conversations with patients and families" (Browning, Meyer, Truog, & Solomon, 2009, p. 905).

The program at Boston Children's Hospital used actors to help practitioners develop relational skills when discussing medically charged difficult conversations. Thus far, the program has been successful by developing practitioners who are able to feel comfortable and confident when having difficult conversations with patients and families.

Another study, which focused on conflict resolution with colleagues in healthcare, looked at numerous sets of data. Specifically, the researchers observed conflicts during high stress events in operating rooms. While some participants in the study argued that the conflicts were beneficial in some circumstances, others relayed that there were negative consequences to the conflicts. While the researchers and participants recognized that conflicts could not be avoided, they did suggest skills so the conflicts could be managed professionally. The researchers suggested many tools we will discuss in later chapters, including compromise, self-awareness, goals, and perceptions (Overton & Lowry, 2013).

The knowledge gained from the field of medicine can influence the field of education. It is important to practice professionalism, research-based answers, and de-escalating a tense situation. Therefore, just as conversations with families are important for practitioners at Boston Children's Hospital or between surgical team members, it is important for teachers to engage in conversations with a variety of stakeholders.

PSEUDO-SYNONYMS

When researching and implementing practices focused on effective communication and difficult conversations, four other terms became evident as "pseudo-synonyms" to the term "difficult conversation":

1. courageous conversation
2. fierce conversation
3. critical conversation
4. direct conversation

Each of these pseudo-synonyms will be discussed. They may also be used somewhat interchangeably throughout the rest of the book.

Courageous conversations are conversations that include both parties being open to learn in order to deepen understanding on a specific topic and in order to make an informed decision. These types of conversations are generally defined as open, learning, and informed. However, when extreme differences arise in courageous conversations, more heated or difficult interactions can result (Rozen, 2015).

Many times, conversations we dread having can be changed from the term "difficult" to "courageous" because it recognizes the fact that it takes courage to engage in the topic or interaction. When engaging in a courageous conversation we may be fearful of the unknown response or reaction, or we may feel as if we are taking a big risk. An example of a courageous conversation is often recorded as a conversation discussing racial differences or cultural divides.

"Fierce conversation" is also a term used when discussing an impending difficult conversation. Susan Scott (2004), a researcher and master teacher, focused on the idea of powerful communication as a fierce conversation.

Specifically, a fierce conversation is "one in which we come out from behind ourselves, into the conversation and make it real" (Scott, 2004).

The idea behind fierce conversations focuses on recognizing our own interpersonal difficulties that directly result in our inability to communicate effectively. Interpersonal skills such as verbal communication, listening, assertiveness, decision-making, problem-solving, and negotiation skills are specifically discussed in relation to fierce conversations.

Critical conversations and/or crucial conversations are defined by many scholars as any interaction where the stakes are high, opinions differ, and emotions are high and invested. Critical conversations in the field of education are defined as interactions between and among students, as well as conversations between coworkers.

Direct conversations have had many meanings throughout the years. However, in the age of technology and Urban Dictionary, the term "direct conversation" has taken on another meaning. It means that a face-to-face conversation is needed because technology communication has led to misunderstandings. Therefore, a face-to-face, direct conversation has the goal of clearing up any confusion because all three communication strategies are viewed when communicating with technology. Going into a direct communication after having a misunderstanding via technology can begin a conversation with high negative emotions. However, the goal is to clear up the miscommunication.

FOUNDATIONAL TOOLKIT

Regardless of the term, this book will provide strategies to engage in difficult, courageous, fierce, critical, and/or direct conversations. Each chapter will focus on a specific relationship topic in the field of education and provide useful strategies and ideas to build your own toolkit as an educator:

- Supervisor/s and Staff/Teachers (Chapter 5)
- Colleagues (Chapter 6)
- Educator (Administrator) and Students (Chapter 7)
- Facilitating Student and Student (Chapter 8)
- Educators and Administrators to Families (Chapter 9)

Each toolkit will have the same foundation:

1. Use interpersonal skills (Chapter 1)
2. Focus on and reduce communication blocks and barriers (Chapter 3)
3. Recognize and control reactions and emotions (Chapter 4)

Specifically, in the following chapters we will discuss how to recognize our emotions, how to be open and honest about our preconceived notions, and how to engage productively in difficult conversations with parties who are willing and/or unwilling to converse. Learning how to recognize and control personal reactions to difficult conversations will help each reader develop a sense of agency when encountering difficult conversations as an educator.

DEFINITIONS

Before continuing to the next chapters, which will focus on developing a professional toolkit, a few terms need to be defined for the purpose of this book.

Coworker: A person who works in the same building or district, generally individuals who have similar roles.

Educator: Anyone in the school building who interacts with students (principal, teacher, classroom aide, administrative assistant, custodian, nutrition worker, etc.).

Family: Includes, but is not limited to, parents, stepparents, grandparents, uncles, aunts, siblings, neighbors, or any adult that is involved in the caring and upbringing of a child outside of the school environment. It is important that educators have a wide view of family, especially with the constantly changing demographics of families.

Supervisor: Someone in an administrator role, such as a principal, dean, assistant principal, athletic director, superintendent, director, etc.

Teacher: Anyone who teaches (provides information or instruction to students) in a school; a classroom teacher.

Chapter 5

Toolkit 1: Supervisor/s and Staff/Teachers

> *"Educators know only too well that teaching is a never-ending learning process. It is less acknowledged that improvement in teaching can be enormously facilitated by quality relationships between teachers and administrators."*
>
> —Vicki Zakrzewski (2012)

The environment and culture of a school building is one of the four foundational blocks built on the backs of the administration, who influence the staff and teachers' morale in a building and district. If the leadership style or the culture of the school (district) building is not built on trust, professionalism, and listening, the overall school (district) culture suffers. Therefore, the school culture and sense of community that a supervisor or supervisors create is essential before a collaborative, communicative environment can be built.

Before diving into strategies of building a strong school culture, there is one important thing to consider—personality traits. While there are many personality trait tests, the one I have found most beneficial for quick reflection is the Personality Compass. The Personality Compass states,

> Everyone has some characteristics from each of the four types, but one will capture the essence of your personality more accurately than the others. This is your dominate type. No one type is better than another, they're all just different.

After completing a short questionnaire, your dominant personality type is revealed: North, South, East, or West. The opposite of your dominant type (South and North, East and West) is the type of personality that you have the "hardest" time working with. North individuals are natural leaders and are goal centered. East individuals are natural planners and are analytical. South individuals are natural team players and are non-confrontational. West individuals are natural risk takers and are free-spirited.

It is important to know and be aware of your dominant personality type and the personality types that are most difficult for you to work with because it provides one more layer to your perception knowledge base. It also helps provide background to teams that may not work effectively together versus teams that do.

After discovering personality types, which are hard to change, the next step is engaging in learning about multiple strategies supervisors can embrace to create a welcoming environment. All four of the strategies discussed in this section build on the concept of the WOO factor—Winning Over Others—which was mentioned in chapter 1. This is accomplished through eye contact, getting to know people, and finding commonalities. The WOO factor can be embraced in relation to colleagues, family members, or students.

The four areas we will focus on include:

1. Understand your role and know your goals
2. Develop trust (Predictability)
3. MBWA (Manage by Walking Around)
4. CF (Critical Friends) (Growth Mindset)

UNDERSTAND YOUR ROLE AND KNOW YOUR GOALS

In your position, what is your role? Is your role to be a mentor? A coach? A supervisor? All three? While these three ideas can overlap, it is also good to know how they are distinctly different roles. A question to ask yourself is: Is my goal to increase quality or judge the quality of a teacher or staff member? Table 5.1 shows the differences between the three roles an administrator may take in the field of education.

Table 5.1. Administrator Roles

Coaching	*Mentoring*	*Supervising*
Focus on specific competencies/practices (new or old)	Develop leaders and provide advice	Ensure that processes are performed correctly, including assessing or evaluating staff

While each of these roles has their individual pros and cons, there is one foundational piece that touches each of them: Trust.

Develop Trust. Developing trust is the glue of all relationships. Trust is being reliable and truthful. Trust, in the field of education, is also the quality of predictability. As most teachers are Type A or North personalities, a sense of control often plagues professionals in education. Part of that control stems from the understanding of personal control. When a teacher or staff member can predict how observations, meetings, conversations, support, and so forth will go, a deeper sense of trust is built.

One step to take, in the vein of predictability, is to have an agenda or predictable nature for meetings, observations, and so on. One example of a predictable agenda for a debrief session was depicted in Figure 1.3.

Another way to develop a sense of trust is to care about your staff. Caring can be shown in many ways; however, one way is through the ability to ask for and take their critiques. An ability to be open and a willingness to be vulnerable display your respect for your staff. One suggestion to move toward the sense of trust and caring is to anonymously ask your staff the questions shown in Table 5.2 and take their feedback as something to reflect on as a professional. Many of the "asks" in this list are qualities we ask for or require of our students. Therefore, lead by example.

Stemming from questionnaires, another type of survey that an administrator can provide teachers and staff is a "Get to Know You" survey. What does your staff like? How do they like to be recognized? How do they like to be provided feedback? What is their personality type? What is their favorite candy? Do they have allergies? What is their favorite hobby? Know the people you are supervising.

Once the surveys or questionnaires are filled out, use the information gathered. When you want to show appreciation, refer to the "Get to Know You" survey. When you implement conversations focused on feedback, use the strategies they document for receiving feedback. Show you care. Show you want to provide a positive working environment. And, just as with technology communication, tailor your communication to the individual.

Manage by Walking Around (MBWA) is a strategy often implemented in the field of business. This includes the boss walking around, having their face known, and creating an environment where staff and teachers do not see the administrator as someone who is untouchable or unreachable but as someone who is on the ground level with them. In education, it is also a way to get to know your students and your school building, and to be part of the everyday community of the school.

The term "Manage by Walking Around" was coined by Tom Peters, a management guru. When coining the term, he was referring to managers spending

Table 5.2. Administrator to Staff Questionnaire

Administrators: Ask Your Staff Do I . . .	Y or N
Help others view mistakes and learning opportunities?	
Smile?	
Meet individually with each staff member to identify ways to help them more effectively?	
Use common courtesies (please and thank you)?	
Apologize for mistakes or for teaching others without respect?	
Confront the issues and not the person?	
Demonstrate friendly, positive, and upbeat behavior toward others?	
Listen more than talk?	
Speak directly?	
Value and model continuous learning?	
Recognize my own limitations?	
Offer chances to take risks?	
Remain curious rather than defensive?	
Model accountability and ownership?	
Meet others where they are and help them move forward?	
Keep an asset-based mindset about people (rather than a deficit-based mindset)?	

a portion of their time listening to problems and ideas of staff members by walking or wandering around an office or plant in an unstructured way. This is an excellent way for a supervisor or administrator to be "seen" in the building.

As an administrator of a building, a great way to implement MBWA is to take a cart on wheels and transform it into your "office on wheels." Have a place to put your laptop or iPad, pens, paper, maybe some treats, a walkie-talkie, and anything else you may need throughout the day. Then, get up from your stationary desk in your office, take your office on wheels, and be IN the school environment. Sit in classrooms, help instruct, be an aide, sit by a student—just be someone who is part of the fabric of a school rather than the missing piece never to be found.

When an environment is built on trust and an administrator is seen in the environment, communication is impacted. Communication will occur more often, it will be natural, and a team mentality will be built. Overall, being in the environment will build the morale of the staff. However, it is important to remember that with great comments can come negative comments or conversations. Refer to the survey and questionnaire items. Follow up, accept negative comments, and respond in a respectful way.

Other effective strategies that build on knowledge learned in previous chapters include:

1. Dressing like you fit in. If you are wandering around on a Friday jeans day, wear jeans. Going around in a suit and tie will communicate, through your clothes, that you are hierarchically higher and more important.
2. Listen actively. Truly hear what your staff is telling you or what you are seeing in the classroom.
3. Reflect on the conversations, which includes responding and following up within an appropriate amount of time (usually within twenty-four hours for email). If there is not an answer, at least provide the steps you have taken in relation to the conversation.
4. If your gender is different from the gender you are supervising, remember what we learned about communication and gender differences (chapter 4). Make sure every voice is heard as equal, regardless of the individual's gender or personality.

Real-Life Scenario

One elementary principal in central Illinois embodies the MBWA. In a brief slide deck, she illustrates her passion for learning, engagement, and being in the building. She focuses on being there for students by engaging in gym activities, eating lunch with students, having fun, and giving awards. She encompasses the love of learning and shares that with the students in her building by doing read-alouds, inviting students into her office to provide individual or group lessons, and becoming part of the overall fabric of the school. This principal also understands the importance of helping and celebrating teachers. When there is a dress-up day for spirit week, she joins in. When there is something to celebrate, she is front and center of planning and supporting. Her staff's morale is high because of the care and trust she has built. She also understands the importance of continually learning. Two areas where she excels is the development of her own PLC through Twitter and embracing the "office on wheels" weekly in her building. Overall her message is to support and most importantly have fun. Lead by example.

Reflection Questions:

- What are the benefits of MBWA? For staff? For the administrator? For students?
- How might the Education Communication Model (chapter 1) be used to describe this type of communication strategy?

Critical Friends Group (CFG). Developing professional and collaborative relationships is also important when weaving the fabric of a school environment. One practice that is often used is called Critical Friends Group, or CFG, which was developed by the National School Reform (www.nsrfharmony.org) and is a great addition to an administrator's toolkit.

What is a CFG? CFGs gather teachers together in a PLC format. However, each time, one participant is at the front and center to have colleagues help develop their practice, focusing on a specific question or goal. Overall, the focus is on the professional needs of the small group of participants, not on the needs of the district or school. What do teachers need for their own development: classroom management, networking, math instruction, ideas for family communication?

During each CFG meeting, which is structured to meet monthly for one to two hours, one participant introduces an issue they would like to help with in their professional practice. The groups usually consist of individuals who have the same interest, but not necessarily the same grade band. Professional practice needs could include restructuring a part of the day in order to meet the needs of students more effectively, implementing new standards, or classroom management procedures.

During the meeting time, one individual shares and the rest of the group, preferably trusted peers, provides honest critical feedback. Additionally, each member has a "job" during the CFG, such as time keeper, facilitator, and so on. However, the presenter chooses the structured format of the session, which is provided by the National School Reform. Overall, CFGs are built on reflection, trust, and a common goal of professional development based on the needs of individual educators.

Benefits of CFGs include trust, collaboration, growth, and an acknowledgment by school staff that administrators care about the professional development of members in the school community.

As an administrator you can build an environment where CFGs are a possibility. While you may not participate in one as an administrator, you have the option of participating as a member on the "same level." Developing a sense of agency and ownership of one's own practice as a teacher is crucial to the overall culture of the school, and CFGs are one more way to engage in that practice.

DIFFICULT CONVERSATIONS

So far, the toolkit has consisted of ways administrators can structure collaboration or learning about staff members. However, with all that preventative, foundational groundwork, it is inevitable that difficult conversations will arise.

While this toolkit is a great place to begin or continue your professional growth as a supervisor, the four strategies listed earlier focus on prevention rather than reaction. In this section we will discuss how to engage in difficult conversations when they arise.

In the role of an administrator or supervisor, difficult conversations can come in many forms. However, in relation to teachers there are three major scenarios:

1. Debrief meetings after an observation
2. Disciplinary action
3. Implementation of a new procedure/strategy unsupported by the staff (i.e., no buy-in)

For each of these, as with any difficult conversation, it is important to remember the brain development and emotional stress hormones that can impact reactions, both yours and your staff's (chapter 4).

Debrief Meetings. Providing a structured format for debrief meetings, as is illustrated in Figure 1.3, is an excellent place to begin observation debrief sessions because there is room for reflection, teachers know what to expect, and concerns can be brought up during the structure of the conversation.

Some common definitions for elements of debrief conversations are:

Feedback: *Positive recognition of a job well done or the constructive criticism of a skill or task that could use improvement.*
Desired Behaviors: *The actions or skills that provide the most effective completion of a task.*
Replacement Behaviors: *New behaviors to replace the ineffective or inappropriate behaviors (i.e., Action Steps/Plan).*

These are also applicable when discussing behavior management of classrooms and school environments (chapter 6).

When providing feedback, it is always a good idea to provide balanced feedback. Find positives as well as areas to improve upon. It may be called "glows and grows" or "strengths and areas of improvement." However, a good practice is either the "sandwich approach" or the "4 to 1" approach. The sandwich approach is often described as sandwiching a negative critique or area for growth between two positive comments.

> Sandwich Approach Example: You did well in the read-aloud today. However, I would encourage you to focus more on the vocabulary. The students did not seem to know what was going on in the story. The activity after the story, however, was very well planned out and I could tell you put a lot of thought into it.

The 4 to 1 approach is similar; however, you focus on four positives or areas of strength for every one area of growth.

> 4 to 1 Approach Example: The planning for the math lesson was very thought out. You had the papers ready and the centers ready. The students seemed to really enjoy the centers, and I could tell they were learning. I saw AJ and Sophia cooperatively engaging in the center, which is great social-emotional development.
>
> The structure you thought out for rotating through centers also worked very well. However, there were some misconceptions that you did not think through when planning for the math lesson. This is one area where I feel more reflection would benefit you in the future. Think through all the misconceptions the students may have so you are ready when they come up.

Regardless of how you decide to provide feedback, make sure to always include both positive and negative comments and follow a structure for the conversation. In the example table (Table 5.3), the positive and negative are named "positive" and "constructive."

Most importantly, do not "control" the conversation with your voice. Let the teacher's voice be heard and listen actively. Constructive feedback is also important to implement. Remember, just because you may not be holding someone down does not mean that you are lifting them up.

Real-Life Scenario

As a teacher I have had many principals. I have had principals who have supported me and are in my classroom constantly, not to evaluate but to participate. I have also had principals who only come in when it is "evaluation season," which was very stressful to me and the students. The principal I enjoyed the most? The principal that respected me professionally, knew my family, and wanted to get to know me and my personality, not just my professional self.

This specific principal was not someone who I would consider "fun," but he supported my practice, guided me into leadership positions that I desired, provided reasoning behind decisions, and supported my voice when there was

Table 5.3. **Examples of Positive and Constructive Feedback**

Positive Feedback	Constructive Feedback
Have specific details of behaviors or teaching strategies. (Provide exact examples. If you have the availability to video record the observation and refer to it during the observation, this is the best way to talk about specific portions of the lesson.)	Be specific and focus on the BEHAVIOR and not on the person.
Explain the impact of the behavior or teaching strategy (rationale and research).	Explain the impact of the behavior or teaching strategy (rationale and research).
Be clear in communicating what is effective or successful (next steps).	Remain calm.
Give recognition for positive behavior (asset-based mindset).	Be selective in choosing only what a person can receive.
	Be selective regarding what is in the teacher's "locus of control."
	Watch for nonverbal cues.
	Listen to the individual's perspective of the behavior and/or situation.

a parent complaint or disengagement from the district level for best practices and developmentally appropriate practice in my early childhood classroom.

He invited us to an annual pool party, developed an understanding of my professional qualities, and was someone who could be a "friend" and an "administrator." He did not attend our staff Christmas parties, but was supportive of "fun" spirit weeks. He found a great balance between colleague and boss. While he did have an angry side, he was also willing to apologize and learn best practices for an elementary building, when he was trained as a middle school educator.

Was he perfect? No. Did I feel respected by him? Yes.

—Early Childhood Educator

Reflection Questions:

- What has been your experience with supervisors? If it was positive, why? If it was not positive, why?

Disciplinary Action. When you think about or begin to plan a disciplinary conversation, your heart rate might go up, your hands may get sweaty, your frustration level might go up.

All of this is normal.

When you think about or begin to plan a disciplinary conversation, your mind may be clear, you may feel energized, and you might feel a sense of purpose.

All of this is normal.

Everyone has individualized responses to difficult conversations focused on disciplinary actions. It may depend on the person you plan to talk to. It may depend on the action you will be discussing. It may solely depend on you or the staff member's personality traits. Regardless, disciplinary action conversations are difficult and inevitable when working with human beings.

Embracing the strategies outlined in chapter 4, as well as the strategies outlined in the observation debrief section, is a place to begin. But what if that does not work? It is important to know your non-negotiables before entering the conversation. It is also important to let the staff member and/or teacher vent in a respectful (nonviolent) way, especially if the disciplinary action will come as a surprise to the individual.

Some questions to ask yourself when planning for a disciplinary conversation:

1. Have you already had a conversation to know "all sides"? If not, start here.
2. What is your goal? Make sure you reach this goal or something similar. Hold your ground.
3. Have you built a trusting relationship with this staff member? If not, you need to take this into consideration when presenting and conversing with the individual.
4. What are your non-negotiables? For example, no cell phones, no yelling, no talking over each other, no name calling.
5. How much time do you have planned for this meeting? Make sure you have enough time, but not so much time that the conversation goes in circles.

When engaging in the conversation, make sure the individual understands this is not a debrief session but a different type of meeting with a different protocol and agenda. It is also a good idea to have another party in the meeting if you are afraid there may be repercussions. During the disciplinary conversation:

1. State that this is a different type of meeting; it is a meeting focused on a concern or problem.

2. State the ground rules or non-negotiables for the conversation.
3. State the problem or concern.
4. Ask for feedback from the individual or have them share their "side."
5. Have a respectful and reciprocal conversation focused on the issue at hand. Make sure to keep a calm tone of voice and redirect the individual if ground rules begin to get broken.
6. Reach one of your desired goals as fact.
7. End the meeting with a polite and respectful demeanor. (Even if someone is being written up or fired, showing respect is key.)
8. Take notes throughout the meeting.

After the meeting, it is imperative to type up your notes from the meeting and send them immediately. This provides the other individual time to see the notes and "agree" to the minutes, and it documents that the conversation was had. Email is best because of the ease of documentation.

Implementation of New Standards, Procedures, Policies. We have all experienced board of education, school board, or districtwide new ideas being pushed down to the school level for administrators and teachers to implement, even if training does not accompany the implementation. There may not be buy-in from the teachers. There may be pushback. There may even be teachers who refuse. However, as an administrator, embracing the concepts and strategies outlined earlier in this chapter to build foundational respect and rapport is key.

It is important to remember that people, including adults, children, teenagers, or any other party, like to have a sense that their voice is heard. That their voice is something that matters. And that their voice can be part of the larger picture—providing that experience can create an environment of 99 percent buy-in compared to 40 percent buy-in of implementing something new.

But sometimes even if staff and teachers don't want to implement something, we still have to! So, then what? Provide choices within your and their locus of control.

Real-Life Scenario

In the state of Illinois, as with many states around the country, Common Core State Standards were mandated from the top down. I was in one of those districts. I was one of the administrators that needed to tell my staff that Common Core was mandated, even though all we heard on social media, news outlets, from parents, and sometimes from other educators was that Common Core was awful. It was not good for our kids and that the math kids were asked to do was ridiculous. I am sure that you saw, as well as I and my staff members saw, the meme of 2 + 2 = 4 and 2 + 2 = 5. (If you didn't, look it up.) We heard nothing but negativity, so my staff felt nothing but negativity.

However, as the leader of the school I needed to make sure my staff was going to implement it with fidelity. So, what did I do? Well first, I complained. But once that was out of my system, I did research. I knew that we did not have a choice. However, what was in my control? In my control was HOW we implemented it and HOW my school culture was built or broken from this mandated implementation.

What did I find out? Common Core was not all that bad, and we did have some flexibility. I began with a small focus group of teachers who I knew were the teacher leaders in the building. We met monthly, talked about the Common Core, researched, and came up with a game plan. We focused on our control.

Here was our choice. We had to implement Common Core, which was not a choice. But did we want to implement it with bad attitudes or positive attitudes? Positive. Did we want to work as a team or individual? A team. Okay, instead of focusing on the negative, we focused on the positive. We gathered every piece of positive information we could find about Common Core. We changed our mindsets and began to get more teachers on board. We began to see the freedom that was available in implementing the Common Core. The availability to move around from expensive curricula and create classrooms that were student centered.

While this process took a while (close to two years), we are at 99 percent of teachers who have bought into the implementation of Common Core. And on those days that someone is having a bad day or can't seem to find anything positive about this top-down mandate, we have others to pick him or her up, debrief, support, and collaborate with.

So, it is possible. It took a lot of work. A lot of listening. A lot of research. A lot of changing mindsets. But it is possible.

—Illinois Administrator

Reflection Questions:

- Was this a positive communication experience or a negative communication experience? Why?
- What, if anything, could have been done differently?
- Can you relate this experience to your own life as an educator? If so, how did your experience compare to this experience?

Administrators lead the school and create the school culture. When they show respect, which has been found to be the most valued quality of a leader, the school staff feels supported and is more likely to stay. Being humble, saying thank you, listening, and sharing the credit are ways for a leader to show respect to the staff in the school building. A TED Talk at a Nevada 2018 event suggested that if you are ten feet away from someone, respect is making eye contact and smiling. If you are five feet away from someone, you make eye contact and say hello. With respect comes stability in the school environment. A building without stability creates a workforce that is less motived, less collaborative, and ruder in all situations.

STAFF/TEACHER TO SUPERVISORS

It is often the case that staff and teachers in a school building have more experience and/or have been in the school building longer than the administrator. While that is not always the case, it is one thing to consider when discussing communication and relationships between teachers/staff and a supervisor.

Overall, it is important to remember that support goes both ways. The supervisor needs to support the teachers in all settings, especially in front of parents, and the teachers need to support the principal, understanding the hierarchy of respect. While disagreements can occur, basing the conversations in norms and respect will take a team a long way.

However, it is also important to note that not all teachers respect their supervisor due to personality or pedagogical differences. When this is the case, practicing patience, respect, and setting norms is imperative.

Real-Life Scenario

I have been teaching for close to twenty years now and have had eight principals. The principal I have now is #7 out of eight. She is disrespectful, she does not implement best practices, and I do not feel supported. I don't even think she has taught elementary before because she does not know what she is talking about. She tries to manipulate staff and students with behavior tactics and incentives, which sometimes work, but come on.

How do I interact with her? I set my own norms. She is not someone who is willing to hear feedback or wants to have any part of teacher input. I set my norms before conversing with her. I set my agenda. I know what I need to tell her, expect pushback, and will settle for less—I have that mindset before going in. I set the bar high and I have a goal that is lower. I support my information with research—quick and to the point. Does she listen? Usually not, but to keep my sanity I must stand up for my students but also know what is expected and what she will most likely allow.

These conversations are difficult. When she first became my principal, I had anxiety attacks. I hated going to work. I felt like I was not serving the students to the best of my ability. But I realized some things are in my control and some things are not. I had to make that realization, set my own norms, reset my mindset and thinking, and just push forward. She will be gone, I will have another one soon enough. She is not the worst, I mean she is seventh out of eight. I have made it through worse, with less support and more demeaning attitudes. My norms, my idea of my own locus of control, and my goal of serving my students to the best of my ability keep it in perspective.

Difficult conversations are hard, especially when you are a "lowly teacher" and your administrator is hard to work with.

Reflection Question:

- Brainstorm ways to work with difficult administrators using many of the concepts discussed in this book.

Chapter 6

Toolkit 2: Colleagues

Communicating effectively with your colleagues minimizes misunderstandings and maximizes work efficiency. Effective communication also produces healthy working relationships and allows you and your colleagues to resolve issues in a collaborative manner.

—Uplift Events (2017)

As with any relationship, coworker to coworker relationships can be fruitful, but they can also be frustrating. For this specific chapter we will focus on teacher to teacher and teacher to specials teacher, as well as relationships and communication with staff members that help run the school building, including but not limited to custodians, secretaries, and other staff members.

For the purpose of this discussion, a specials teacher could be any of the following: assistant teacher, co-teacher, reading specialist, physical therapist, occupational therapist, speech therapist, or other personnel who enter a classroom to help in the development of a student. Regardless of the relationship, the main objective is getting to know your colleagues and developing a common goal—often student centered. While the focus of student growth is usually the combining factor, avenues to reach that common goal often differ. These different avenues to reach a common goal are often where difficult conversations come into play.

Preventative ways to build trust and respectful relationships are very similar to those outlined in chapter 5 for administrators to get to know their school staff. Get to know each other, understand working styles, and most importantly keep conversations respectful and keep "gossip" out of the school building.

STAFF MEETINGS

For administrators, one way to decrease off-topic or difficult conversations is to have an agenda for a meeting. Staff and teachers also have a role during meetings.

During staff meetings or grade-level meetings, disagreements may arise. The most important first step in these situations is to set norms. Often, norms, or common understandings of how communication will transpire, are built as a group and can be implemented in and out of the group setting with individuals. Common norms for meetings or discussions include:

- Developing a common goal and ensuring that discussions focus on the common goal.
- Listening activity: Respect others when they are talking by making eye contact and having no other distractions (i.e., phones).
- Speaking from your own experience (no generalizations).
- Using "I" statements when stating something or expressing feelings.
- Not being afraid to respectfully challenge one another (make decisions, not personal attacks).
- Participating to the fullest of your ability. Community growth depends on the inclusion of every individual voice.
- Being conscious of body language and nonverbal responses; these can be just as disrespectful as words.

Once norms are set, discussions in meetings can begin. Be willing to get out of your comfort zone. Consciously expand your conversation circle to include coworkers who do not share your perspective. A wider conversation circle is important because when we leave our comfort zone, we can encounter experiences that challenge previous perceptions about the world.

As part of this process, recognize all the individual funds of knowledge within your workplace and community. This includes getting to know your coworkers and recognizing the positive impact they have on the school community. Everyone brings something positive to the school building. Finally, a common mindset of compromise is imperative to build. However, compromise does not always work. Therefore, having a designated or logical leader to ensure that conversations stay focused and a decision is made is also important.

SPECIAL/EXTRACURRICULAR TEACHERS

While every teacher is special, in this section we will discuss how teachers can co-teach/plan with teachers and professionals who come into the classroom or take students out of the classroom for various needs. An important concept to remember, which is often difficult for North personality-type teachers, is the ability to give up control and listen to other perspectives.

Conversely, for specials teachers who enter a classroom or engage with students, it is important to respect the teacher and develop a relationship with the teacher. Overall, each person who engages with the students needs to understand individual goals for each student and for the overall classroom.

What if there is a disagreement between the teacher and a specials teacher? It is essential that the disagreement does not impact the students' experiences and that the students are unaware of the disagreement through interactions seen or conversations heard. Then, the ethics of teaching come into play. First, direct the concern respectfully to the person. If you do not feel that the problem or concern is solved, bring in a mediator to help in the goal-setting and compromise session. Overall, each conversation, especially one concentrated on difficult conversations, needs to base interactions in norms, as described earlier.

Timeliness can also impact feelings and thoughts about coworkers. If it is your time to pick up your students at 11:05, show up at 11:04 to ensure that you are on time. Everyone has a schedule, and everyone is busy; therefore, showing respect through timeliness can prevent potential animosity.

Real-Life Scenario

A few years ago, when I was teaching kindergarten in a charter school, I had several specials teachers come into my classroom or pull students out for remediation. One of the specials teachers was the ELL teacher. She worked with at least ten students in my classroom, so we decided that what would work best is for her to come in during our center, focused learning time and work with her students on specific concepts.

The first week went well. She showed up on time, I had a folder of things that we were working on that I provided her, and the students were flowing through the centers well. However, that was the honeymoon stage. The next week and the weeks after she missed days without notification, which messed up my schedule for the students. When she did come in, she sometimes would focus on the information I had provided, and sometimes she would not. Again, with no reasoning or conversation.

As a passive-aggressive person I made the folder brighter with very specific notes for her regarding the concepts we were working on. I talked about her behind her back to release my frustration, and overall nothing changed. Eventually, her supervisor and my mentor stepped in. She mediated a conversation between the two of us. We both used "I" statements, were able to see the other person's perspective, and ended with a compromise. I recognized that she often had other things come up that prevented her from coming into my classroom.

However, she did not realize how unprofessional and disrespectful I saw this action as being, especially without her notifying me that she would not be in my classroom. We compromised that she would inform me if she would miss and that she would make sure to concentrate on the activities I provided. On the other hand, I would have other things for the students to do in case she had something come up.

While the ending worked out well, the path to get there was frustrating.

Reflection Questions:

- What could have been done differently to ensure positive communication?
- How could this teacher incorporate the Education Communication Model (chapter 1)?

STAFF AND TEACHERS

A common saying among educators is that every teacher should become best friends with the secretary and the custodian. While this might be hyperbole, the underlying meaning is solid. In many school buildings the secretary "mans the ship" and ensures that students have a tardy slip, parents are not sent to classrooms to have "meetings" during instruction time; they are also the gate-keepers for substitute teachers. Custodians, on the other hand, ensure that your classroom is clean, help run the school building, and are the "keeper of keys."

While the secretary and custodian are often seen as arguably the "most important" people in a school building, developing strong relationships with all staff members is another foundational block in running a school smoothly.

Many of the same strategies can be used as already described. However, sometimes it is hard to get to know everyone and to know what is happening in everyone's life if there is a big staff.

Real-Life Scenario

As a first-year teacher I had many things to think about and try to remember each day. I was overwhelmed and going through a divorce, which was taking up much of my mental capacity. It was dictated to staff through an email blast one Monday morning at 7:30 a.m. (which is the same time students arrive) from the head cafeteria worker that if our lunch number was not posted outside our door by 10:00 a.m. then we would have to sit with our students until the end of lunch, because they would need to make lunch for the students.

Essentially, they only made enough hot lunch for students marked on the sheet, and if we didn't mark that number our students would suffer, and we would have to sit with them until their lunch was made. I did not read this message before my lunch break and did not post my number by 10:00.

I walked my students into the cafeteria, sat them down, and began to walk away. The head cafeteria worker yelled across to me that I needed to sit with my students. Not knowing what she was talking about, I said, "No, I am going to lunch." She responded saying, "I told you that if you didn't post you would be punished with your students." This did not set with me well. I whipped around, looked her in the eyes, and yelled, "You do not tell me what to do. I am leaving my students here. It is my lunch time," and I walked out. Everyone in the cafeteria saw, and only a handful of colleagues knew I was high-strung from the divorce proceedings.

While the secretary came in to tell me during my math lesson that I needed to see her after school, in quite a stern voice, I never did. The cafeteria worker and I never had another conversation, and my students were not punished anymore. What happened behind the scenes? I do not know. Was this handled appropriately? No. Did I know what was going on in the life of the cafeteria worker? No. Did she know what was happening with me? No. Was it solved? I think so. However, reflecting on this I would have handled it differently, while also holding others accountable.

Reflection Questions:

- How might you engage in this situation if it happened to you?
- What are some ideas that could have been used to communicate more effectively?
- Could the Education Communication Model (chapter 1) have been used in this situation? Why or why not?

As a coworker and colleague it is important to remember:

- How you treat people defines you.
- Incivility (rudeness, offensive jokes, texting in meetings) can decrease the mutual respect in a work environment. Remember, perceptions are reality.
- Some people are toxic. Reflect on your work life. Are you the toxic person? Are your coworkers toxic? Engage in strategies that decrease communication but still create a respectful environment. (Remember the old adages: "Be the bigger person" and "Kill 'em with kindness.")

Chapter 7

Toolkit 3: Educator and/or Administrator to Student

The student is not giving me a hard time; the student is having a hard time.

—Anonymous

A strong classroom and school community/culture is essential to student growth and establishing a feeling of safety. In this chapter we will discuss developing a classroom culture from a culturally responsive lens, focus on the importance of teacher language, mutual respect, logical consequences, problem-solving, understanding challenging behaviors, and various teaching styles that influence communication on the path to building a safe school environment.

However, before diving into the different sections, we will discuss a way to build an overall foundational positive feeling in the school and classroom. While there are many strategies, the strategy we will discuss focuses on a structured morning meeting. During the morning meeting time in the schedule, which should be one of the first things students engage in, every student hears their name in the classroom environment or school building, thus providing a sense of "I belong here."

The structure of a morning meeting is part of the Responsive Classroom management system, which also incorporates logical consequences, discussed in this chapter. There are four parts to a morning meeting, and every part is essential to creating a welcoming, safe, and caring environment for students to develop a sense of trust when difficult conversations inevitably arise.

1. Greeting: As part of the greeting, every student hears their name in the classroom or school environment, engages in the action of eye contact,

and builds a sense of community. When students feel safe with the educators/administrators and students, risk-taking, problem-solving and overall learning can occur at a higher level.
2. Share: The share is a part of the morning meeting that can be completed in several ways. It is a time when students can share about their lives, others can ask questions, and a sense of community and family is built.
3. Game: Again, there are various games that can be played during this time. However, the goal is to build a sense of camaraderie and friendship based in trust.
4. Message: This is when the teacher shares information about the day to be transparent and open.

Every school day should begin with these interactions as a preventative measure to arguments and/or difficult conversations. The next step to building trust and mutual respect is how you, the educator, speak to students.

TEACHER LANGUAGE

How you speak to students influences their brain development. As mentioned in several other chapters, brain development is impacted by stress hormones, which can be triggered by negative language. Specifically, for students, the prefrontal cortex is impacted by communication and behavior management techniques (see the "Logical Consequences" section that follows). Therefore, language is powerful and can make or break the classroom/school environment for a student. It is important to remember that, yes, teachers can bully students, consciously or unconsciously, using language.

One reflection that is often incorporated into professional development focused on teacher language is having participants think of two instances. First, they are instructed to think of the kindest thing a teacher ever said to them. Second, they are asked to think of the meanest thing a teacher ever said to them. Through this activity, participants often can remember verbatim the meanest thing, while they often relay a "good feeling" about a teacher who encouraged them. This activity illustrates the importance of language and the impact of negative language in someone's life.

So how can every educator and reader of this book become a teacher who is the "kindest" teacher and not the "meanest" teacher? Engage in mutual respect (see below) and focus on teaching styles that involve mutual respect.

There are four main types of teaching styles. The goal for all educators and administrators should be one of mutual respect, which encompasses the mentality of "Let's do this together; we all have something to learn from each other." This collaborative type of teaching is called authoritative. The other types of teaching styles do not create a safe environment. There is the authoritarian style that is often described as "Do what I say because I told you to do it." Students behave because the teacher displays bully characteristics and the student is fearful of repercussions.

Another teaching style is defined as a teacher who doesn't care or know what to do. This is a permissive teaching style. Classrooms with this teaching style have students who do not feel safe because there is limited to no structure, which students crave. Finally, there is the indulgent teaching style, which rewards students for doing everything. In these classrooms, students behave solely based on the understanding that they will get something for their good work or behavior (i.e., sticker charts, candy, etc.).

Positive language and an authoritative teaching style create a positive environment for all students, which leads to the feeling and action of mutual respect.

MUTUAL RESPECT

Trainers who focus on the concept of mutual respect often hear the comment "Well, the students do not have any respect. They are not respectful to me, they are not respectful to their parents. They are just entitled." A trainer's response? "I would like to push back a little. When a student doesn't know how to read, what do we do? Teach them how to read. When a student does not know how to add or subtract, what do we do? Teach them. Well, when a child does not know how to behave, what is the current practice? We punish and reprimand. Why don't we TEACH them and not just state or model?"

So, how do *you* create a mutually respectful environment? Design a lesson plan that teaches what respect is or what behavior is expected.

Overall, mutual respect is "a feeling that something or someone is good, valuable or important, shared between two or more people. We believe that respecting the people who keep us safe is an important part of this value. We care for each other's thoughts and feelings." Mutual respect is possible for every educator in every classroom and for every administrator in every building with every student. It takes time, patience, a willingness to help a student's brain develop through repetition, and reflection to ensure that what you say or do to students would be acceptable if they did it in return—hence mutually respectful.

LOGICAL CONSEQUENCES

Mutual respect leads to the idea of behavior management systems that encourage and support students' brain development, specifically through logical consequences. In this section we will discuss logical consequences and why engaging in the behavior management system of logical consequences builds the foundation of mutual respect. However, first we will discuss further the brain development of students.

The prefrontal cortex is the part of the brain that is essentially at your forehead. In this portion of your brain you develop impulse control, problem-solving, making connections, focusing and organizing, and ignoring external distractions. This part of our brain does not fully develop until our early twenties. Therefore, students in our classrooms are a long way from fully developing this part of their brain. Hence, it is our job as educators to ensure that our language, consequences, and interactions help develop positive relationships in the brain rather than negative ones.

That being stated, logical consequences, as compared to behavior charts, punishments, or time-outs, help develop the prefrontal cortex. Logical consequences should be the goal of classroom management systems because when a student has a disciplinary action that directly relates to the misbehavior, the prefrontal cortex builds deeper connections for cause and effect.

So, what is a logical consequence? "Punishment that fits the crime." Essentially, if a student misbehaves, the consequence should logically connect. What you will notice, however, is that not every "misbehavior" is bad or intentional; however, there is still a "consequence" for the action. Table 7.1 provides examples.

Table 7.1. Logical Consequences

Misbehavior	Logical Consequence
A student continues to break their pencil.	Provide them with a golf pencil that cannot be broken.
A student draws on a desk/wall/locker.	Provide the student with the materials to clean up the item.
A student knocks over a tray that another student is carrying.	The student helps pick up the tray.
A student waves scissors around.	The student cannot use scissors the rest of the day. (Make sure to provide a time when the student can show you they know how to appropriately behave.)
A student touches other student when lining up.	The student stands next to the teacher.
A student is not engaged in an activity that is needed for mastery.	Ask the student, "What do you think will help you do better with ___?"

The most important thing to do when implementing logical consequences is to state, "I see that you made the *choice* to _____; therefore, you will need to make a different choice. Do you want to choose ____ or ____?"

Incorporating logical consequences and choices (no more than two that the teacher can live with) into classrooms develops a link between the misbehavior and the consequence, which in turn helps develop the prefrontal cortex. The idea of choice, by stating to the student "It is your choice," when a logical consequence is given develops a sense of autonomy.

When engaging in logical consequences, it is important to remember the guidelines.

1. Ask the student to help choose (put the consequence in the form of a choice).
2. Make sure the consequence is logically connected to the misbehavior.
3. Only give choices you can live with as the educator or administrator.
4. Keep your tone of voice firm and calm.
5. Give the choice one time, then act to enforce the consequence. (Do not get into a power struggle.)
6. Expect testing, but be consistent (this helps with brain development also).
7. Allow the student to try again (do not hold a grudge).

UNDERSTANDING MISBEHAVIOR

When engaging with students in classrooms and school buildings, it is great to have a plan in place and preventative measures. However, does this get to the root of the issue? No. It is also important to understand the behavior and the "why" behind the behavior—in other words, the function of the behavior. However, before understanding the function, the form of the misbehavior also needs to be identified.

While part of this process is identifying the form and function of the misbehavior, the other portion of the process is getting to know the students, understanding what is happening in the lives of the students, and understanding that some students have not developed the coping strategies to express emotions in socially acceptable ways. Also, we must understand that students can have bad days just like all of us.

What are challenging behaviors? They are behaviors that:

1. cause injury to self or others
2. cause damage to the physical environment
3. interfere with learning new skills

4. socially isolate a student
5. are inappropriate for the age or cultural background of the student
6. are challenging for educators or family members to manage

There are five overarching categories that define forms of misbehavior including: aggression, tantrums, noncompliance, social withdrawal, and self-injury. Each of these forms one of three functions (or a combination of functions): obtaining something, escaping something, or causing self-stimulation. Each form and function will have a different response, usually including the process of teaching a replacement behavior (coping strategy). However, it is important to understand that you, as the educator or administrator, do have some control of the situation once these foundational pieces are understood.

When students feel supported, heard, and cared for (mutual respect), difficult conversations and misbehaviors will decrease.

REPLACEMENT BEHAVIORS AND SOCIAL STORIES

When students misbehave, educators need to understand the form and function of the behavior. However, it is also important to identify a replacement behavior. It is not useful to name a behavior that "cannot" be allowed if something does not replace that behavior. This is often discussed when people are trying to stop a behavior, such as nail biting or smoking. That behavior has become part of their life; therefore, instead of engaging in that behavior, something needs to replace it, such as sucking on a cough drop or eating food.

In the classroom, this is also important. If a child routinely yells during whole group time or stands up during a lecture, this behavior needs a replacement behavior. As an educator working with other stakeholders, a replacement behavior can be discussed, taught, and reinforced.

Telling someone (a student) "no" does not solve the problem. Helping the student replace the behavior with a "more acceptable" behavior is the key to teaching and active communication.

One way to engage in teaching replacement behaviors is using social or structure stories. While social stories are often referenced in special education services, they are also a great tool for any student, in any classroom setting. Some individuals may define social stories as a

> tool that supports the safe and meaningful exchange of information between parents, professionals, and people with autism of all ages. The people who develop Social Stories are referred to as Authors, and they work on behalf of a child, adolescent, or adult with autism, the Audience. (Gray, 2018)

Other individuals define social stories with a wider definition: a "highly effective way to teach social norms, routines, and skills," including replacement behaviors in a classroom. Notably, though these may be more effective in elementary classrooms, middle and secondary educators can take these concepts and make them applicable to their experiences.

The key areas to remember when developing and designing a social story include:

- The title should be descriptive.
- Pictures of the student should be included in each picture.
- Replacement behaviors should be stated (short and sweet). Could be printed as a bullet-point list for a reminder throughout the day.
- One should acknowledge that mistakes might happen.
- Students should know that they can do the replacement behavior and be successful.

CULTURALLY RESPONSIVE PRACTICE

Mutual respect can be met through many avenues. One of those avenues is through culturally responsive practice. Culturally responsive teaching or the practice of engaging in cultural responsiveness is using the cultural knowledge, prior experiences, and performance styles of diverse students to make learning more appropriate and effective for them; it teaches to and through the strengths of these students (Gay, 2000).

Through this process the students see themselves in the classroom, increasing accountability, responsibility, and ownership of the classroom, as well as validating the experiences of students. Overall, "the goal of culturally responsive teaching is to create a learning environment conducive to all students, no matter their ethnic, cultural, or linguistic backgrounds" (Frey, 2010).

Foundational understandings of a culturally responsive classroom focus on relationships and the concept that learning is both a cognitive and social emotional process, at all grade levels. There are four pillars for culturally responsive practice (Osher, Sidana, & Kelly, 2008):

1. Safety
2. Support
3. Social Emotional Learning
4. Engagement and Challenge

These four pillars also support or can be supported by other concepts discussed in this chapter and other chapters of this book.

In addition, part of culturally responsive practice is understanding how students communicate. For example, how do students use technology to communicate and stay informed? Understanding the current terms for communication is essential to bringing culturally responsive practices into the classroom, as well as continuing to develop the concepts of mutual respect.

For example, at the time of writing this book, students interacted or communicated using Snapchat stories, Instagram stories, WhatsApp, and Twitch, which focuses on interacting with gamers. Young users have decreased their use of Facebook and Twitter in recent years. It is also important as educators to engage with students on platforms they are comfortable with and engage with daily. Instead of staying in the "archaic" avenues of communication, such as email and Facebook, engage in up-to-date, innovative communication.

Building a positive and inclusive classroom community can be challenging at times. However, with structure and consistency, a positive environment will be beneficial for the social emotional growth of students. Additionally, building a mindset and culture of acceptance is significant. In recent years there has been discussion regarding tolerance versus acceptance. In this book we will discuss the idea of acceptance. Tolerance has a more negative connotation, while acceptance is viewed as being more positive and welcoming. The idea is that tolerance leads to statements of "I will just tolerate you" versus a statement associated with acceptance such as "I accept you in my community regardless of whether we are the same or different."

Positive classroom communities also include effective communication strategies and welcoming aesthetics (e.g., inclusive posters). Another way to talk about positive classroom communities is through the term "inclusive classrooms." Inclusive classrooms are classrooms that are "friendly, caring and supportive, and that let students explore the relationship between material and personal and social experiences" (Yale Poorvu Center for Teaching and Learning, 2018, para. 1).

It has been found that teaching methods that do not help students connect to their personal lives are often ineffective for learners outside of the majority culture, thereby resulting in more disengagement and possible misbehavior (Wlodkowski & Ginsberg, 1995, p. 147). So, how can educators ensure that classroom environments are not solely aimed at the majority culture but are inclusive for all students? Develop norms and expectations of positive language in the classroom.

DISCUSSION

Interactions between educators/administrators and students are important for the overall environment. Teachers and administrators will inevitably have difficult experiences or conversations with students; however, mutual respect, choices, and preventative measures are the best ways to ensure that classrooms are not overrun with difficult conversations. Understand child development, understand brain development, and understand where the student is coming from to decrease judgmental and confrontational conversations.

Real-Life Scenario (Administrator to Student and Family)

Context: During one of my first years as a school administrator, I worked with Madison. Madison was a middle school student who had been at our school for several years. Madison struggled with her behavior—she was incredibly bright but spent much of her time in class, chatting with her peers, arguing with her teachers, and barely completing her work. This new school year was different, though. Madison was making better choices in class, and all the adults supporting her were excited, especially her mother, who worked closely with the school to monitor and support Madison's success.

One day Madison's teacher told me there was technology missing from the classroom, she was pretty sure Madison was at fault, but didn't have any concrete evidence. I brought Madison into my office, asked her about the situation, and she denied any wrongdoing repeatedly. After interviewing a few other students, who all said it was Madison, we decided to check her backpack. Madison opened her bag for me and showed there was nothing there.

I called Madison's mom that night to share our concerns about Madison's role in taking the technology. Madison's mom was very angry with me, telling me that I was accusing her daughter of something she hadn't done, and I wasn't giving Madison credit for changing since the previous years. Madison told her mom she didn't steal anything, and her mom said she believed what Madison said. I acknowledged her concerns but was frustrated since several students had said they'd seen Madison with the technology. I ended the conversation by telling her mom I just wanted to make her aware in case something showed up at home.

The next day a student came to me and told me that Madison had told her she had the technology. She said that Madison had brought it back to school in her backpack to show off that she did take it. When the class went to the bathroom, another administrator and I checked her bag, and there was the technology. I called Madison's mom to let her know I needed to meet with her about the situation. She was very upset but told me she would be at the school soon.

Before the Conversation: I had a few minutes to prepare for the conversation, and knew I needed to think carefully of how I was going to address the situation with Madison and her mom. I was aware that her mom was angry with the school and felt that Madison was being blamed because of her past behavior. Mom also believed Madison told the truth, and I knew she would be disappointed when she found out Madison hadn't been truthful. I knew my goals for the conversation had to be:

- Getting Madison to tell us what happened
- Helping Madison's mother understand why I had to administer the consequence stated in our family handbook
- Preserving the relationship I had built with Madison's mother

I was very apprehensive about this final goal because I was concerned that administering the consequence would ruin the good work Madison had done and my relationship with the mother.

During the Conversation: Madison's mom came into my office with Madison and was very angry. I asked Madison to wait outside so I could have an opportunity for her mom to unload all her feelings and thoughts to me without Madison being present. I expected Mom would need space to process and wanted Madison to see the result of that processing, which was that her mom and I would hopefully be on the same page.

Once Madison stepped out, Mom looked at me with a look of exasperation, threw her hands in the air, and said, "Alright, tell me how you know she did this when she's been doing so good." My immediate gut reaction was to put the evidence on the table, but I realized I needed to attend to the relationship first. So, I began by thanking her mom for coming in. I named how critical our partnership was for supporting Madison and stated that I knew how excited everyone has been for her progress so far.

I told Mom that I was apprehensive about this conversation and hoped that we would be able to come to an agreement and continue to work together to support Madison. Madison's mom immediately relaxed—I could see her shoulders drop. She then said, "I get it, I do. I appreciate that. I am just so tired of her always getting blamed for things. Can you tell me what you know?"

I then gave her mom the facts—exactly what had happened—and then showed her the technology from Madison's backpack. Her mom stared at me for a moment, then got up, threw open my office door and demanded Madison come in to my office. As soon as Madison came in, she looked at me, looked at my desk, looked at me again, and her eyes widened.

She then spent a few minutes trying to come up with an explanation—telling us all the reasons why she was innocent and how she had been framed. Eventually, her mom put her hand up, told Madison to stop, and looked at her and said, "I am sick of your lying. I am so sick of your lying." She then turned to me and said, "What's the consequence, Ms. Ivy? It is good enough for this."

My heart immediately went to Madison at this moment. I knew how angry her mom was, and that the anger was no longer directed at me, but her daughter. I knew how much trouble Madison would get into outside of school and how important it was for Madison to remain invested in school, believe in herself, and know that she could come back from this choice.

I looked at Madison's mom and told her the consequence as set forth in the handbook. She took a deep breath and asked if there was anything I could do to soften the consequence. She looked at Madison and back at me and shook her head. She said, "It's been so much better. I can't have this get worse again."

At this point in time I directed my conversation to Madison, because of her age and because of the level of responsibility I needed her to take for the situation. I asked Madison her thoughts on the consequence. Did she deserve this and why? She sat for a minute, looking at her mom and me, and agreed she did deserve it. She then explained why, looked down with tears in her eyes, and apologized to her mom. Madison's mom and I both expressed appreciation for each other, and I told Mom we'd met again in a few days to ensure Madison was back on track.

Result of the Conversation: Madison served her consequence for stealing school property. When she was done, I met with Madison and her mom and she apologized again. My relationship with Madison's mother wasn't damaged in any way by the conversation or consequence. Madison's behavior fluctuated for the rest of the year, but she did not steal anything again.

Reflections: This conversation was a difficult conversation that turned out in a pretty positive way. I had already had many poorly planned and poorly executed conversations with parents before this one. My ability to empathize with both Madison and her mom was critical to the conversation. I believe the conversation was successful because my priority was maintaining the relationships with Madison and her mother, not doling out a punishment. In my busy day, I could have just called Mom, told her I found the technology, and administered the consequence over the phone. But I couldn't do that and feel right about the conversation. I am so glad I didn't.

—Krysten Ivy Wendell, principal

Reflection Questions:

- Was the Education Communication Model used? If so, how? If not, how could that be engaged in this situation?
- Reflect on each part of the scenario. What stands out to you as a professional? Why?

* Information in chapter 7 and chapter 9 can be interchangeably applied to administrators and teachers.

Chapter 8

Toolkit 4: Student to Student

> *Communication is an important skill for every modern student to master. Advances in digital media, changing career landscapes, and greater competition in colleges and workplaces makes improving student communication skills a must.*
>
> —A. Anntar (2018)

A solid and positive classroom culture is essential to building a foundation for a productive, collaborative classroom. When students feel a sense of accountability and ownership in the classroom, they feel a sense of community and family. When they feel safe, supported, and respected, they are more likely to participate in respectful communication, even when difficult or argumentative conversations arise.

As an educator and/or administrator, teacher language and the mutual respect students receive jump-starts the foundation for a classroom that is built to engage in polite difficult conversations. This concept was outlined in chapter 7.

Once the foundation is built, the next tool in the toolkit includes continued work toward a sense of community. Some ideas include creating a class contract or class-made norms (aka rules), developing the daily routine of classroom discussions, and engaging in the practice of learning how to problem solve respectfully and effectively.

However, before diving into the strategies, as the teacher/educator in the classroom, it is important to evaluate your teaching methods: Are the teaching methods in your classroom student-centered or teacher-centered? Do you engage students in their learning or do you lecture most of the time? Our goal as educators is to be more student-centered with the teacher as facilitator, which will be evident in the descriptions that follow.

CLASS CONTRACT/CLASS-MADE NORMS

Developing a contract with students' input is important to developing an understanding of how everyone will treat everyone else in the classroom. When classrooms engage in collaborating on developing class contracts and class norms, a reflective classroom community is built. A reflective classroom community is a place where rules are explicit, and accountability is developed to protect everyone in the community, regardless of perspectives. While this concept is focused on student-to-student interaction, the teacher needs to deliberately plan and nurture the process of developing the contract and norms.

The process of developing a contract or norms can be accomplished through four simple steps.

1. Define what a contract is and what norms are.
   a. Contract: Implies that all parties have a responsibility to uphold the agreement.
   b. Norms: Rules or expectations that everyone in the classroom will follow in order to create a safe and trusting environment.
2. Ask students to reflect in order to develop a class contract and class norms.
   a. When have you felt uncomfortable?
   b. What is a pet peeve of yours?
   c. What makes you feel safe or trust others?
3. Develop the contract and norms (brief).
   a. Brief and to the point.
   b. Mutually decide on consequences if parts of the contract are not followed, focusing on the concept of logical consequences.
4. Initiate the contract and norms.
   a. Sign and hang in the classroom to engage in whole class accountability.

Reviewing these four steps, you may be thinking to yourself "What is the difference between norms and a contract?" That is a legitimate question. While some people see them as distinctively different, as stated above in number 1, others see a contract as the method used to develop classroom norms. Whichever your view, going through this process will help interactions between students be respectful, trustworthy, and open.

DAILY JOURNALS AND INTERACTIONS

One study found that individuals are more willing to share information when they are writing a journal-like entry. This effect is the same as individuals feeling more confident on the other side of a computer screen than they are face to face with someone else. Regardless of the individual nature of the self-reflection through journal writing, vlogging, or blogging, the act of reflecting can transform and develop individual mindsets (Lindsey, Roberts, & Campbell Jones, 2004; Buehler, Ruggles Gere, Dallavis, & Shaw Haviland, 2009). Therefore, engaging a version of journal writing in combination with face-to-face discussions has the potential to build on the positive foundation of respectful communication in a classroom environment.

Face-to-face conversations can take many formats, however, using the structure of text protocols, which are also part of the National School Reform website as discussed in chapter 5 (Critical Friends Groups). Text protocols, as defined by the National School Reform, are powerful and effective in groups that engage in facilitated discussions. Protocols provide a structure that is followed in order to share ideas, discuss similarities and differences, and respectfully communicate with peers.

Engaging in these groups or journaling activities daily builds a classroom environment where students feel safe to share and provides multiple opportunities for students to discuss ideas. Furthermore, the quality of the discussions is important and can build off the text protocol structures. Additionally, providing prompts that are open-ended will develop a culture where experiences and opinions matter and can be discussed respectfully.

One specific type of interaction that builds a classroom of trust and respect is the daily morning meeting, which is outlined in chapter 7. Morning meetings are based in the Responsive Classroom management system and have four parts: greeting, share, game/activity, and message. Completing these four sections every morning provides an environment of acceptance, ownership, and belonging. During the greeting, it is important for everyone to hear their name in the classroom, creating a sense of community. It is also important to engage in eye contact and social skills accompanying introductions and greetings.

The share portion of the meeting can be completed in several ways, including each person sharing one thing, people signing up to share, or three people volunteering to share. Part of this is to develop a sense of community. Once each person is done sharing, encourage the class to ask questions to gain more insight about their peers in their classroom. As an educator myself, I have completed this activity with preschool students through adults in professional development sessions—each group of participants/students has enjoyed this activity and has found value in creating a welcoming environment.

PROBLEM-SOLVING

As discussed in another toolkit, embracing mutual respect and logical consequences in a classroom and school environment also helps create problem-solving skills for students to engage in respectful conversations, even when viewpoints or strategies are not congruent.

Problem-solving and engaging in difficult conversations are essential for students as they move in the world. An activity that can be used at any grade level is one of the Standards of Mathematical Practice, specifically number 3: Construct viable arguments and critique the reasoning of others.

The third standard is one of the eight foundations of mathematics, but it can be implemented in many other parts of the classroom. Therefore, bringing this activity (Figure 8.1) into math class and then extending it to other parts of the day is one strategy for helping students develop norms and engage in conversations with different perspectives. The way to initially use the activity is for students to complete math problems and describe their methods, which often differ from those of their peers.

Therefore, engaging in these "math talk moves" or sentence starters is a way to learn how to have productive conversations with different points of view. When taking this discussion technique out of the math block, some of the words will need to change—such as "strategy" to "viewpoint" but the concept is a solid foundation.

DISCUSSION

The practice of knowing how to engage and implement strategies with students and between students with different points of view is a fundamental skill needed in the workforce today. Implementing these practices into a classroom environment provides a road for students to follow throughout their lives. Turning away from a teacher-centered classroom to a student-focused classroom is the impetus for small group discussions, interactions, and difficult conversations. What better place to learn how to interact with others than in a classroom setting that is meant to be a place of learning, reflection, and growth?

Math Talk Moves	So, what I hear you say is…
I agree with your answer because…	I disagree with your answer because…
My strategy is like yours because…	My strategy is different because…
Could you explain it another way?	I don't understand…
How do you know your answer is right?	What is another strategy we could use to check?

Figure 8.1. Math Talk Moves

Chapter 9

Toolkit 5: Administrators and Educators to Families

Good two-way communication between families and schools is necessary for students' success.

—American Federation of Teachers (2007)

Building solid partnerships with families is crucial to a positive classroom and school environment. Families are essential to the equation of positive environments because there should be a partnership between home and school. In this chapter difficult communication will be discussed, specifically how to engage in preventative actions, such as home visits and positive phone calls home, as well as other types of communication, such as parent–teacher conferences, newsletters, and/or websites.

Regardless of the communication, it is important to remember to stay open, available, and respectful, and to view your role as a customer service representative, providing solid structure and sometimes education to the families you work with. Note the word "with." As administrators and educators, we work "with" families, not against or above them. Therefore, this chapter will discuss strategies that you as an educator and/or administrator can use to ensure that relationships are built on a solid foundation of "we" rather than "us and them."

One other concept to understand before diving into strategies is the difference between family engagement and family involvement. The goal of schools needs to be one of family engagement. The terms "involvement" and "engagement" are often used interchangeably when discussing family-school-community collaboration. However, the two terms are defined differently.

Engagement focuses on working with all the involved stakeholders, such as families and community members, in a mutually beneficial relationship

(Child Welfare Information Gateway, 2016). Involvement, on the other hand, is when the school plans events and then invites the families or community members to attend without investigating stakeholders' goals or talents that could facilitate activities.

While schools and educators strive for engagement, research does support the idea that any increased parental interest and support of students can help them both academically and socially. However, most research states specifically that family engagement can produce even better results—for students, for families, for schools, and for their communities:

> A school striving for family involvement often leads with its mouth—identifying projects, needs, and goals and then telling parents how they can contribute. A school striving for parent engagement, on the other hand, tends to lead with its ears—listening to what parents think, dream, and worry about. The goal of family engagement is not to serve clients but to gain partners. (Ferlazzo, 2011)

There are many strategies and activities that help educators and schools become more focused on engagement rather than on involvement. In the activities described, the reflection of involvement versus engagement needs to be kept in the forefront to truly understand how to help families feel like their voice is heard and valued.

WELCOME BACK NIGHTS AND HOME VISITS

One of the first ways to begin the school year with positive communication and relationships is to bring the family into the school. Help the family feel welcome and let the family see where the students will be for most of their school day.

Before the school year begins, it is important to have a back-to-school night where families can meet the teacher, see the classroom, and join to eat a meal. Eating a meal together is a foundational activity that many families around the United States no longer embrace. Therefore, eating a meal together during the back-to-school night has the potential to bring families closer together, creating a happy memory in the school building, as well as providing stability and connectedness for the students. During the mealtime, administrators and educators might plan conversation topics, family games, or just leave it open to conversations between and among families and the school staff.

Aside from the back-to-school night, home visits are also very important for building a positive view of school and creating a sense of "family" or welcoming. Both educators and administrators can participate in home visits.

However, it is important to remember that home visits can be completed differently depending on the area, school, or district. Regardless of how the home visit is completed, research shows that educators entering homes and getting to know families in "their territory" increases student attendance and builds a strong foundation for positive communication between families and teachers.

While home visits can take many forms, it is suggested that home visits happen before the school year begins or within the first few weeks. At these visits it is important to set the expectations for the school year and to complete an interest inventory for the incoming student with the family. An interest inventory can have several questions on it, but generally the teacher wants to get to know the student and family through the inventory to understand the student's and family's funds of knowledge.

Another idea for a home visit may involve providing home kits that include various games or information for the upcoming year that will help the family and student engage in learning at home. While this primarily depends on the age of the student, books or other activities could be provided for older students.

Home visits are specifically important in early childhood grades, for students or families who are new to a district, or for families who have not had good experiences with the school system for various reasons. As administrators and educators, initially building positive relationships and experienceswith families develops a positive view of the school from the family's perspective. Additionally, "home visits can give teachers the insight they need to help all students succeed" (Education World, 2016, para. 2).

Home visits are also specifically important in school districts with low-income and/or immigrant or refugee families who may have a history of negative experiences with schools or who may be intimidated by the school system in general.

One school district in Sacramento, California, founded the Parent-Teacher Home Visit Program (PTHVP) in 1998. This program

> trains teachers to make home visits to families that will build relationships and foster parent-teacher collaboration focused on improving student achievement. At the elementary school level, home visits take place in the fall and spring. At the end of the first visit, teachers invite the family to come to the school and they develop a plan to communicate throughout the year. The second visit occurs just before spring testing. (Henderson, 2011, p. 16)

Other school districts have similar strategies for implementing home visits. For example, Early Head Start and other preschool programs that focus on birth through five years old have their own protocol for visiting families beginning prior to the birth of the child. Another example is from a national charter school that requires all teachers to make home visits prior to the start of the school year, with the goal of setting a positive tone and helping students feel more comfortable on the first day of school.

Additionally, through anecdotal accounts of home visits, teachers have reported that students are excited to show teachers their rooms and their overall home. In these same anecdotal accounts, teachers have reported being invited to dinner and having whole family experiences that tend to provide teachers with insight into the culture and life of a family. Overall, home visits are beneficial to the foundation of a positive and collaborative partnership for the school year.

In the Mindshift podcast, the hosts investigated the impact of home visits on students' improved learning in the classroom. The hosts found, through interviews, that parents and teachers alike have feelings of intimidation, caring, and pushback. Families may feel intimidated that teachers want to enter their homes, but they understand that the teachers care and are trying to build a positive relationship. Teachers are intimidated by entering homes—something that is not a common practice—and feel the pushback from parents not wanting them to enter, stating the fear of "checking in" on them. However, the relationships that are built during home visits empower everyone involved.

The most important activity during a home visit, as outlined by the Mindshift podcast, is focusing on hopes and dreams. What are the hopes and dreams of everyone in the life of the student?

Foundations to School–Home Communication

1. Positive Phone Call. While we already discussed home visits as a positive first step to open communication with families, so is the implementation of a positive phone call to every parent within the first couple weeks of school.
2. Individualized Communication Method. Each family finds different communication styles appropriate for their lifestyle. As early childhood educators building the foundation for positive school–home relationships, it is useful to understand what families consider the most appropriate way to communicate. During the home visit interest inventory and discussion, deciding on an effective communication strategy will be beneficial for the school year.

PARENT–TEACHER CONFERENCES

Parent–teacher conferences are also a great time for educators to build a foundation of "us." During parent–teacher conferences it is important to have

Table 9.1. Parent–Teacher Conferences

Parent–Teacher Conferences *Focus on Relationship Building and Sharing*	
What is "seen"?	What is "heard"?
– Structured schedule (displays preparedness and provides the family with a sense of where the conference is going). – Student work (shows progress).	– Student's voice (student-led conferences). – Positives and areas for improvement. – Ask for family input. – Thank the family for coming.

a structure to follow and encourage the student to participate (student-led conferences). While planning parent–teacher conferences, it is also important to think about engagement versus involvement. Are you providing times that work for the family? Structure and time flexibility display to the families that you have planned, that their student is engaged in their personal growth and learning, and that you respect their voice and ability to participate.

While parent–teacher conferences can look different for each grade level, here are some ideas to incorporate. They allow you to be proactive in building a foundation so that when difficult conversations inevitably arise, trust and respect have been established.

NEWSLETTERS AND/OR WEBSITES

Why are classroom newsletters important? They keep families engaged and informed. Why are school newsletters important? They keep families engaged and informed.

Although each family may want to be communicated with in various formats, it is important to make sure that all the information communicated is in a written form. This can be through a weekly newsletter and/or a constantly updated website. Whatever form is chosen, it is important to remember that families are busy; therefore, provide information using the fewest words and provide pictures to help families remember upcoming events or information addressed.

Additionally, make sure that all written communication, or any type of communication, is in the language that is most comfortable for the family to understand (do not use Google Translate). Finally, along the lines of customer service, providing information in multiple formats based on a family's needs and wants is important. Maybe some families only check an app provided by the teacher or only look at printed copies of information. Provide the information in the most accommodating way for the family, which will prevent communication pitfalls.

Some suggestions for creating an effective newsletter or website message include:

1. Short and sweet (bullet points of need-to-know items).
2. Announce new content only.
3. Add pictures to support the content.
4. Next steps for families. (What do you need the families to do with the information?)

SPECIFICS FOR ADMINISTRATORS

While administrators can do many of the items listed above, the administrator arguably sets the tone for the whole building. Therefore, the administrator needs to not only support educators' efforts to preemptively communicate with families, but he or she also needs to practice whole school initiatives. Whole school initiatives can be twofold: (1) engage families; (2) provide impactful and effective professional development to educators. This will prepare them and train them for difficult conversations or other difficulties that may arise in the field of education or in their school specifically.

Administrators to Families. Administrators who support back-to-school nights, impactful parent–teacher conferences, and are a welcoming face at every event create an atmosphere of "I feel welcomed here" or "I belong here" for the students and families. Additionally, administrators who support the work of the families and really listen to families can create an environment where families feel respected and support the safe school environment.

However, if a concept or concern cannot be addressed, it is important for the administrator to treat the family with respect and provide reasoning and possible replacement activities. When an administrator does not display mutual respect for families, school communities can crumble.

Below is a vignette of an ineffective, disrespectful communication dialogue between a principal and parent (exact emails, names changed).

Real-Life Scenario

Email from Parent 1:

Dear Mrs. S (Principal),
 Hello! I hope you are doing well. We are excited going into the new school year! I am very concerned, however, that the 4th graders are again losing

lunch recess. I know my son, as well as many others, is heartbroken over this. I'm wondering if punishing the entire grade is fair. Tomorrow is Miles' birth, and this has completely ruined the thought of coming to school. Is the cafeteria shorthanded? Do you need people to volunteer to come in and help maintain the noise level?

Miles is incredibly upset that he and other classmates are being punished for the actions of others. When I asked what happens when they do not get recess, he explained that the kids are stood in the hall and "yelled at" about the past behavior. (I'm sure no one is yelling.) How long are they stood in the hall?

I would like to be part of the solution in getting this resolved. I am firmly against recess being taken away, but I understand there must be consequences for not following the rules.

I will be at lunch tomorrow to see if I can understand better what is happening. It is very disturbing for me to think about how many children struggle through the rest of their day because of this.

Thank you for taking the time to read my concerns.

Respectfully,
Parent 1

Email response from Principal:

Good Morning,
We always appreciate help, but they are warned 3 times about noise level before recess is taken away.

Mrs. S.

After receiving this response, Parent 1 reached out to Parent 2 for support.

Email from Parent 2:

Good morning Mrs. S.,
Mrs. Parent 1 forwarded me the communication regarding recess she has communicated with you. She forwarded this email to me because of my profession, research, and overall advocacy and determination that all children, including the students at School Name, are being treated with respect and staff are implementing developmentally appropriate practices. Unfortunately, I see (and hear from my own son also) that is not occurring, specifically with the 4th graders at School Name.

While we love School Name, this is very disheartening. We are entrusting our students will be treated with respect, however they are losing one of the most important parts of the day, causing undue stress to students who are "behaving" and, as research shows, is causing more distress to the students who are constantly misbehaving.

Overall, I also have a concern about "whole class" reprimands/punishments and the taking away of recess. I am sure you are fully aware of the benefits of recess for all students and how whole classroom punishments are not developmentally appropriate for any age, but especially for elementary aged students.

However, I have heard that when a whole class is talking or doing something that is not following the rules, they are punished as a class, including the taking away of recess, which creates a bigger problem rather than teaching students how to follow the rules and procedures of the classroom and school building. When students are unable to release energy, just like adults need to release energy talking to each other, looking through their phones, etc. it creates a brain that is not ready to hear or learn.

I am sure that once sharing this with your team and other members of the staff, appropriate trainings and/or changes will be made. If you need help thinking of suggestions, please let me know. If you need some research and/or articles to help other staff members understand the importance of recess, being outside, getting energy out, and the detrimental impact of taking away recess in order to "teach" the students how to behave, please let me know and I will be more than happy to share with you appropriate information.

Finally, as a professional and a parent at your school, I would truly appreciate a full emailed repose or in person conversation regarding this concern. I would hate to end our time at School Name with an issue that is causing undue harm to my child and the rest of the students in the building.

Thank you,
Parent 2

Response from Principal:

Dear Parent 2, thank you for email concern. Yes, I will aware of the research on brain breaks. This was why we scheduled into an additional break in the afternoon. They did not lose the full recess but 5 minutes out 15. They have been warned for last two weeks. The lunch ladies can hear if they want apple or oranges it is so loud. We had to do the same with second grade. It is now down to one class. Some students cannot eat when it is so loud. It will work its self out.

Response from Parent 2:

Good evening Mrs. S.,
  Thank you for the response.
  However, it is quite disappointing that an educator who knows the research would state that "it will work itself out." This is an unacceptable way to handle the situation. If "working itself out" includes well behaved students crying, being upset, and not desiring to come to school—this is not working itself out for everyone.
  If this is a known problem, as you stated, then the solution you and your teachers/lunchroom workers have figured out is not working. If you are aware of the research in education, I would hope you would engage in more positive interactions rather than interactions from educators that are in many ways considered bullying students into behaving. Do you know why the students are being loud? Do you know if they all can state why it is important to be quiet? Have you TAUGHT and not just told or modeled the appropriate ways to behave? Can you name the students that this is negatively impacting? I can, and I am not in the building.
  As the leader of the building being able to know the impact of teachers' actions is imperative to building the foundational aspects of both academics and social interactions. If students are yelled at, they learn that yelling in school is acceptable. If students only behave because of fear of losing something, they are not learning the intrinsic value of academic and social growth. Thinking about the teachers working with the students in the lunchroom, have they considered how their interactions impede their relationships with the students?
  A school building should be built on mutual respect, not one of fear to behave. As one of the top elementary schools in Town I would hope that you would be a role model and disengage in the practice of taking away recess when there are multiple other ways to engage in the learning experience of social interactions and eating in a social atmosphere.
  As you stated, you know the research. As I stated, my son who is never in trouble (along with many other students) who comes home and hate lunch and have cried during the day when only in the lunchroom because of the disrespect they experience from adults. It is unacceptable when students are learning the negative ways adults interact with students, especially when adults can engage in much more conducive experiences and languages.
  As stated before, I would be more than willing to come in and help teachers understand. While this impacts my son, it also will impact many students that come in and out of your doors as an elementary school. I will do this for free because I care about my son's school and the experiences the students in your school engage in. I also know that Parent 1 has offered to help during lunch, a person that many of the students know and trust.

The practice of taking away recess is not a policy in the School District and is detrimental to the health of the children you are watching over every day. It does not matter if it is 1 minute, 5 minutes, or the whole recess, the process of managing through fear is unacceptable.

Please let me or Parent 1 know if you would like our help any further.

Please also respond to this email so I know what my next steps need to be in order to get this situation solved before it gets more out of hand and causes more damage to the social and academic atmosphere at School.

Thank you,
Parent 2

Principal Response:

Parent 2
Yes, we have modeled for all grade levels. Fourth grade is the only one notable handle this. I mean working itself out, is the short absence of recess will calm it down and the people that are still having a problem with work with the family core. If that does not help, then their lunch time will be switched, and their teachers will watch them in line. Mrs. Mason is always welcome to help in our building as I stated last week.

Mrs. S.

Parent 2 Response:

Good morning Mrs. S.,
I am disappointed at your response and your blatant disregard for my WHOLE email. Since it is apparent, we are not going to be able to have a professional and collaborative relationship to not only benefit the 4th graders, but the other students and professionals in your classroom, I have one request.

I am now documenting and letting you know that if my son misses any part of recess, I request that you, Classroom Teacher, and/or the teacher who takes the time away from my son calls both my husband and I to explain the circumstances of what my son did to lose any part of his recess time.

I have offered professional development. I have been professional and polite. However, your responses are brisk and unresponsive to the full concern.

If this does not happen, the phone calls, I will make sure to contact your supervisor with the documentation we now have between the two of us regarding this situation.

My phone number is: ###-###-####
My husband's number is: ###-###-####

Sincerely,
Parent 2

Reflection Questions:

- What are your initial thoughts and feelings while reading this scenario? Why?
- If you were the administrator, how might you have engaged in more effective communication?
- As the parent, how might you have engaged in more effective communication?

ADMINISTRATORS PREPARING EDUCATORS

Administrators who support educators in their building and district can also build or destroy the strong foundation of a school environment. One way administrators can support educators, aside from the suggestions above, would be to create impactful feedback and learning cycles for educators to practice engaging in difficult conversations.

Two examples, from my own research, include emails from hypothetical parents and mock parent–teacher conferences. While both take time, professional development and the iterative cycle of the adult learning theory with these professional development experiences have proven to increase teacher confidence and a sense of agency when engaging with families.

Hypothetical Emails. As part of professional development (and undergraduate courses), participants receive various kinds of emails from family members. All the emails are real and are based on submitted emails from fellow or former teacher colleagues. Once a participant receives an email, they have twenty-four hours to respond in a respectful way. (Email etiquette dictates that twenty-four hours is the appropriate time frame to expect a response.) This can also be done face to face.

As part of this activity, participants must provide research and/or a tip sheet with next steps, while also not engaging in any communication blocks, which is where peer feedback comes in. As participants respond to the emails, peers provide feedback on the tone that is perceived and the quality of information and next steps. After participating in this process several times, educators begin to feel more confident and are more aware of their written (or verbal) tone as perceived by others.

Below are three examples of emails; as a professional you may have experiences to pull from also:

Ms. _____,
My son continues to come home saying that kids are being mean to him. Today he came home with a bite mark. Why did I not get notified? Are you going to kick the other kid out? There should not be any biting.
Christine

Ms. _____,
My daughter has started biting a lot at home. She is biting her sister, she is biting her dog, sometimes she bites me. Is she doing it at school? Do you know how I can make her stop?
Christine

Ms. _____,
As you know my husband and I are going through a divorce. I would rather you not tell him anything about our kids. I will do that. He is a jerk and he doesn't need to hear things from you.
Christine

Mock Parent–Teacher Conferences. Mock parent–teacher conferences can take many formats; however, the impact of practicing how to have difficult conversations with families prior to engaging in a difficult conversation is important and can be transformative.

One way to engage in mock parent–teacher conferences is to set up scenarios, much like organizations or preparatory programs set up mock interviews. Scenarios are provided, interactions are had, and reflection and learning are created. A second way is to engage in virtual learning environments, which is a new and innovative practice in the field of education.

What is a virtual learning environment (VLE) and how do you use this to engage in the practice of parent–teacher conferences and difficult conversations? VLEs incorporate the professional development (e.g., difficult parent–teacher conferences) with "real-life" situations in a simulated environment. These experiences offer safe, flexible, and appropriate training conditions to practice pedagogical skills. In this environment, teacher candidates are coached, paused, and given real-time feedback rather than after-the-fact feedback.

Additionally, in the VLE there are avatars that can provide real-life responses, interruptions, questions, and answers. The research on VLEs indicates that there is a nine-second suspension of disbelief, which means that after nine seconds teacher candidates feel as though they are teaching in a

TEXTBOX 9.1.
VLE PARENT–TEACHER CONFERENCE MOCK SCENARIOS

PARENT–TEACHER CONFERENCE SCENARIOS
EARLY CHILDHOOD

Goals:

Engage the parent/guardian
Inform the parent of strengths and areas of improvement
Close the conference with areas to work on together

Scenario 1: (Teacher-Candidate Information)

Sarah Jones is a four-year-old girl in your classroom. She will turn five in time to be in kindergarten in August. You are really working with her on school-readiness skills. She stills needs to work on some social and academic areas. You have briefly spoken to her parents before, but also know that her parents are having difficulty at home and are planning to get divorced. Sarah has three siblings, all of whom are younger than her. Sometimes when Sarah comes in to the classroom you can tell she has gotten herself ready for the day and is sometimes very tired and sleeps through the morning.

Scenario 2: (Teacher-Candidate Information)

Sergio Martinez is a three-year-old boy in your class who enjoys playing in the dress-up area, doing puzzles, and is very friendly and nice to all the students in the classroom. He also has very good manners. This is his first year in preschool and the first parent–teacher conference his mother is attending. She does not know what to expect, but also knows that her husband is not happy with Sergio putting on "girl" clothes in the housekeeping area. While you are aware of this concern, you want to focus on social and academic areas that home and school could work on together.

Scenario 3: (Teacher-Candidate Information)

Monica McCampbell is a five-year-old girl in your classroom. She did not make the age cutoff for kindergarten last year but will be going in August. She is the oldest in the classroom and is excelling beyond her peers academically and socially. In the conference you want to discuss areas to keep her progressing in a classroom that is not really on her level. You want to discuss ways you could provide her extension work. You are not sure her parents will be willing to help her at home with homework since they have the view that in preschool she should not have homework. During the conference your goal is to help them understand the importance of having homework to help her stay challenged.

Scenario 4: (Teacher-Candidate Information)

Maria Patal recently immigrated with her parents. They all speak English well but do not understand the American school system. They want to see homework, worksheets, academics, and no playing during the day. They do not understand the importance of play in the American preschool system. Maria is also very quiet and does not explore the classroom during playtime. During the conference you want to try to help the parents understand the importance of play and provide ideas to get Maria to engage in play. You are not concerned about her academics. You would like her to make more friends and engage in creative play in the classroom.

---

real classroom rather than in a simulated classroom (Dieker, Hynes, Hughes, & Smith, 2008).

While VLEs can be used in many formats, engaging educators in the practice of informing families of difficult matters or engaging with an aggressive family member is beneficial and builds teacher confidence when the real-life experience occurs.

Below is a sample of mock scenarios (Figure 10.2), but many more could be created for the demographics and situations in your school and community environment. There is the option of basing the situations on real-life situations.

At times educators may need to have a difficult conversation with a family. As with any difficult conversation, this can cause anxiety and fear. Many people often try to avoid difficult conversations or conversations that may be more conflict based or argumentative (Stone, Patton, Heen, & Fisher, 2010). However, teachers have a responsibility to communicate with families on many topics (Graham-Clay, 2005).

Communication is key to a collaborative, respectful, and professional relationship. However, at times teachers find themselves in situations where conversations or communication styles become difficult or uncomfortable for one or both of the parties involved. Therefore, it is important that teachers have experiences and guidance to develop a toolkit of skills focused on addressing difficult conversations with families, as well as administrative support.

DISCUSSION

Overall, families are important to the life of students and to the life of the school. It is important to consider all family types and make sure that communication is occurring in a way that is most effective for each family. Just as educators are asked to individualize lessons to students, it is important to individualize communication techniques to families. Most importantly, it is important for the educator to stay calm, even if the parent is not.

Real-Life Scenario

"Ms. Mayfield, umm, somebody's mama is in there beating on her ass."

Ignoring the fact that my second grader just used a curse word, I said, "What? What is happening?"

By that point another student came out of the bathroom and said, "Yeah, Tanisha's mama is in there beating on her."

Stunned, I yelled into the bathroom, "Girls, out!" I needed to get my kindergarten students out. I then ran to the administrator's office that was next door and said, "Mary, she's beating her."

Confused, Mary, the curriculum coordinator, came out and said, "What?"

Rapidly, I said, "A mom, she is in there beating her kid."

Mary ran into the bathroom and approached the mother. I did not enter also; I stayed out with the kindergarten students. I could hear some of the conversation.

"You can't do that here," Mary said, as she and the girl exited the bathroom with the mother behind them.

Walking up the stairs to the office, the mother was on the heels of Mary and the student, yelling, "You can't tell me what I can or can't do with my daughter. I can punish her however I want!"

What happened next? I do not know. I do know, however, that the mother was not reprimanded, and the child was not protected. What would I have done? Called the police and told the parent she is not allowed in this school building because we keep our kids safe. Did that happen? No. I am disappointed, but I know that I was in fear and don't know what I would have done if I was in an administrator position.

I was glad to have an administrator to push the situation onto. And I was very impressed that Mary never raised her voice, she focused on the child, and got her to the office. However, I did not see the continued support of safety.

That experience made me reflect on my job, my position as a teacher, and my students. I need to keep them safe, but how do I do that if I am fearful of a parent who enters mad, aggressively, or combative—either to me or my students? I still do not know what I would do.

Reflection Questions:

- Put yourself in the shoes of the teacher. How might have you reacted?
- Put yourself in the shoes of the administrator. How might have you reacted?
- What thoughts, feelings, and questions do you have after reading that interaction?

* Information in chapter 7 and chapter 9 can be interchangeably applied to administrators and teachers.

Chapter 10

A Research Study

Education, Technology, and Knowledge Sharing Communities

> *ECOT (Electronic Community of Teachers) is a virtual community of practice where teachers who might otherwise be isolated in their classrooms can share experiences, identify best practices, and forge new relationships.*
>
> —Brazelton and Gorry (2003)

This chapter is an addendum. If you, as the reader, are seeking research focused on technology, communication, and the use of knowledge-sharing communities, then this chapter is for you.

Before the creation of the Internet, veteran or retiring teachers would pass down binders, tubs, and sometimes closets full of information for new/novice teachers. However, as generations of teachers continue to evolve, information sharing and technology are increasingly linked, which provides a worldwide information-sharing community. Specifically, for teachers this has changed the way planning, collaborating, and brainstorming happen.

There are multiple sources for teachers to access tools, supplies, conversations, or ideas, including, but not limited to, email listservs, message boards, Teachers Pay Teachers, Pinterest, Facebook, Twitter, and Google+. Some researchers and educators have begun to describe interactions of sharing via the Internet as developing a knowledge-sharing community (Brazelton & Gorry, 2003). These knowledge-sharing communities are increasingly becoming some educators' only professional learning community, while others are using knowledge-sharing communities as just one more way to collaborate and gain information.

Knowledge-sharing communities, with social media, are a phenomenon that has grown in the last five, ten, and even twenty years. The first wave of knowledge-sharing communities began when social media first launched in 1997, specifically chatroom discussions. However, at that time in history, people in society did not have Wi-Fi–enabled devices or Wi-Fi available everywhere.

Almost ten years later, in 2006, Facebook and Twitter became available, which was when social media really began to take off in personal and professional groups (Hendricks, 2013). People began using social media in their everyday lives because the Internet, smartphones, and constant access to anyone in the world became possible through the introduction of accessible Wi-Fi. Today, nearly twenty years after the first social media site was launched, social media is considered a "must" by some for the purpose of professional networking and, for some teachers, lesson planning, classroom management, and blogging.

Social media platforms are continually being designed and promoted as places where participation and interaction are easy, accessible, and encouraged. These include whiteboard collaborations, Google forms, Dropbox, YouTube, and podcasts. Additionally, companies such as Slack have begun to spring up to help people collaborate through technology. The use of social networks through technology provides a unique experience for users, an experience not seen or possible in the past (Di Gangi & Wasko, 2016).

As social networking and the Internet continue to grow, so do the terminology and definitions. The term used in research and professional communities to describe Facebook, Twitter, Pinterest, Edmodo, and other social media outlets is "social networking sites" (SNS) (Kio, 2015). "The word 'social' in social networking sites reflects an intention to foster communication longitudinally among friends and families, such that the need to stay connected with them can be achieved through this platform" (Kio, 2015, p. 138).

LITERATURE REVIEW

Due to the relative newness of technology and social media sites, specifically in the teaching profession, there is limited research focused on the topic of social networking in the field of education. However, with the isolation factor and the mentality of sharing knowledge without reinventing the wheel, the education system is a prime place to research, gather data, and understand the evolving use of technology to grow professionally. Educators are in a prime place in history to utilize technology and social networks to collaborate and engage with one another across the nation and world.

Researchers have conducted studies that focus on teacher-to-teacher interaction (Krutka & Carpenter, 2016) using social media; however, most of the research has been conducted in other parts of the world, such as Australia, Pakistan, and Malaysia. There is minimal research focused on U.S. educators. However, the scholarship gained from studies outside of the United States can help inform future studies.

In a study conducted in Australia, researchers focused on pre-service teachers' use of Facebook and e-portfolios to enhance their professional growth (Kabilan, 2016). The researcher in this study found that by using social media, specifically Facebook, many of the ninety-one participants benefited in five areas, which included community practice, professional learning and/or identity, relevant skills, resources, and confidence (Kabilan, 2016).

The study conducted in Pakistan supported the findings found in the study conducted in Australia. The researchers in Pakistan found that educators used social media to gain professional development. Overall, the researchers found that "social media can be instrumental in enhancing the performance of teachers" (Khattak, Batool, Saleem, & Takrim, 2016, p. 127).

Finally, the research conducted in Malaysia focused on teachers' professional development using online blogging (Nambiar & Thang, 2016). The researchers found that teachers were able to be more reflective, share doubts and struggles, and develop ideas or skills to manage students and classrooms. While the researchers did not draw the conclusion that blogging directly contributed to the teachers' professional development, the positive outcomes of blogging and the use of social media were apparent in the findings (Nambiar & Thang, 2016).

While much of the current research surrounding teachers' professional development using social media is being produced by countries outside of the United States, the United States has contributed to some of the available scholarship. For example, in 2014, researcher Emma Hardy examined the spaces educators were creating for themselves using social media to become autonomous learners and, for some educators, educational activists (Hardy, 2014). However, as stated earlier, there is minimal research from the United States focused on social media platforms in the field of education.

SIGNIFICANCE

The trajectory of social media use since 2014 has skyrocketed. Teachers are not only creating a space for learning, but also are engaging, conversing, and planning together around the world. Therefore, this research study aimed to add to the scholarship from around the world as the evolution of social media and professional development continues to evolve, specifically for educators.

While there are many avenues for using social media in the classroom, such as engaging students, connecting with families, or building a website, the purpose of this study was to focus specifically on the professional development and the professional learning communities of teachers using social media. However, since this was a pilot study, other information became available during the data analysis process.

In this study, teachers from around the United States were surveyed and questioned regarding their use of social media to help plan and implement lessons, design classroom management procedures, and organize their classrooms; this included any other topic they might have found useful while using social media.

The results of this study showed the trend in a technologically advanced profession and a profession that has learned to make SNSs work to share, collaborate, participate, and support each other across the nation and world. A small portion of the results describe pushback to the idea of free and open sources for everyone. Regardless of the differing opinions, the findings will be discussed.

THEORETICAL FRAMEWORK

The foundational theory used in this study was the Social Media Engagement (SME) theory, which was originally designed for the business profession when discussing interactions between a user and an organization (Di Gangi & Wasko, 2016; Prahalad & Ramaswamy, 2004). The SME theory was developed by researchers who predicted "that the user experience, encompassing both the social interactions among users and the technical features of the social media platform, will influence user engagement. User engagement will, in turn, positively affect usage" (Di Gangi & Wasko, 2016, p. 2). Essentially, "the SME theoretical model outlines distinctions separating the factors that form the user experience, user engagement, and usage" (p. 3).

Other researchers have supported this idea by finding that the more frequently users participate in activities on social media platforms, the more valuable the platform becomes to professional fields (Kankanhalli, Tan, & Wei, 2005; Li & Bernoff, 2008). This theory was used to understand how, why, and how often participants engaged with SNSs to plan and collaborate with other professionals.

LIMITATIONS

As with any study, there were limitations. The first was that the researcher reached out to individuals about their use of social media. While the purpose of this study was to focus on social media, the researcher also recognized that some of the population was missed by only using technology. There are individuals who use social media less frequently but do use the Internet to brainstorm activities like workbooks and planning books.

Additionally, the researcher unconsciously assumed that all teachers had access to social media and the Internet. Retrospectively, this was an unfair assumption to make. Low-income schools do not always have the technology to support the use of social media to develop professionally. Or educators may choose not to use social media in their personal or professional lives.

METHODOLOGY

Overall, the purpose of this research study was to investigate how practicing teachers in the United States utilize technology, specifically social media outlets, to collaborate or brainstorm their own professional development and classroom environment. Some of the areas could include planning, classroom management techniques, creating activities, providing examples, or just simply asking a question for feedback. Because this was a pilot, fact-finding study, the two guiding questions were open-ended and flexible:

1. How are social media networks used in your professional life?
2. Why is social networking useful or not useful in your professional life?

Procedures

The participants were recruited through social media sites and through email communication. While this focus on technology-based recruitment was useful, it was also an additional limitation, as discussed above. The participants were recruited through self-selection, convenience, and snowball sampling.

Specifically, the researcher reached out to former colleagues, former teacher candidates at a state university, and individuals on Facebook and Twitter using educational hashtags. Some of the hashtags included #teachers, #earlychildhood, #elementary, #secondary, #educhat, #iaedchat, and #iledchat. The hashtags were useful because when another person searched or used that same hashtag, all the information with that same hashtag became available to that person. Therefore, the hashtag was utilized because of the wide-reaching nature of hashtags on social media sites. For example, anyone who added #elementary to a tweet would also be guided to my hashtag post asking teachers to participate in a voluntary survey.

The two social media outlets used for recruitment, Twitter and Facebook, were specifically chosen based on the knowledge that they were, arguably, the two sites that began and sustained the technology phenomenon worldwide. The hashtags were presented on social media, specifically Twitter and Facebook, every other day for one week.

The following three weeks the researcher retweeted the hashtags one time per week. In total, the posts were made six times on both social media sites. An email was sent to former colleagues and previous state university teacher candidates with a sentence asking the email recipient to pass on the link to the survey to other educators.

Once the participants pressed on the link, they were asked to consent to the research. After consent, they were directed to a short, fifteen-question survey focused on their use of social media to plan, implement, and overall engage students in their classrooms. Additionally, the participants were provided with the definition for social media before responding to the online survey. For the purpose of this study, social media was defined as forms of electronic communication (such as websites) through which people create online communities to share information, ideas, personal messages, and so on (Merriam-Webster Dictionary).

Information included on the survey focused first on the demographics of the participant, including gender, age, and years of teaching experience. The survey then included qualitative, open-ended questions for the participants (educators) to answer regarding their professional use of social media. It should be noted that questions on the survey were not designated as "must answer" questions. Therefore, some participants did not answer all the questions.

Data Collection

Twenty-four participants completed the survey. In Table 10.1 the reported demographics are detailed. Additionally, all the participants were in the central time zone.

Other background information questions for participants included the type of school participants taught in, how long they had been using social media, and their comfort level with using social media and/or technology.

Overwhelmingly, 83.3 percent of the participants teach/taught in public schools, while one participant reported teaching in a parochial school, one participant reported teaching in a charter school, and two participants reported teaching in a private school. The self-reported data also included how long each participant had been using social media in a professional manner. This information ranged from two to nine years. Nearly half (47.8%) of the participants had been using social media for ten or more years in a professional way.

Table 10.1. Participant Demographics

Participant Demographics			
Gender	Age Range	Ethnicity	Years of Teaching
Female: 100%	25–30 yrs. old: 4.1%	White/Caucasian: 91.7%	1–5 yrs.: 8.3%
Male: 0%	30–39 yrs. old: 54.2%	Hispanic or Latino: 8.3%	6–10 yrs.: 25%
	40–49 yrs. old: 29.2%		11–15 yrs.: 33.3%
	50–59 yrs. old: 12.5%		16–20 yrs.: 12.5%
			21–25 yrs.: 12.5%
			26–30 yrs.: 8.3%
			31–40 yrs.: 8.3%
Total Number of Participants: 24			

The next set of background questions asked the participants to report their comfort level with technology and social media. Over half (58.3%) of the participants reported that they are very comfortable with technology and could usually solve a problem that arose. A smaller group (29.2%) stated that they know some things about technology but would need to ask for help if a problem arose. Participants were also asked about their comfort level using social media in this pilot study. Nearly three-fourths (75%) of the participants reported that they either use social media for most of their planning or use it one to two times per week for professional planning purposes. A small sliver (8.3%) reported that they did not know social media could be used as a professional planning tool.

After the information was gathered through the pilot study survey questions, the researcher began to analyze the results using the process of open coding. The researcher, through this process, found three themes. The themes will be discussed in the "Findings" section.

However, it should be noted that while the findings are not generalizable, the results add to the limited scholarship available regarding social media use among educators, specifically in the United States. Additionally, the responses are rich with information and can begin to tell the story of how teachers engage with social media as professionals, while also helping researchers and tech mavens know what teachers find beneficial or nonbeneficial on social media.

FINDINGS

Using open coding, the researcher found three themes. The themes were purpose, connections, and overwhelming. Additionally, the founding themes were able to answer the two guiding questions. As a reminder, the guiding questions were:

1. How are social media networks used in your professional life?
2. Why is social networking useful or not useful in your professional life?

The themes of purpose, connections, and overwhelming were apparent in all the participants' responses. Specifically, the themes of purpose and connections could be directly linked to the first guiding research question. The participants reported having a purpose to their use of social media networks. They reported that they used social media networks to connect with other teachers and families.

While each participant identified many social media sites, each also specified what exactly they used the site for in relation to their classroom. This relates to the theme of purpose; there was a useful professional purpose for each of the sites. The theme of connection was also apparent when each participant stated that their goal was to either connect with families and/or other educators. However, the participants were also asked about the pitfalls of using social media professionally. The theme that addresses the second half of the second research question (social networking site that is not useful) was the idea of being overwhelmed with information on social media sites.

Purpose

The purpose theme of using social media sites reiterates the philosophy in the field of education that there is no need to reinvent the wheel when there are available resources at your fingertips. The idea of purpose was evident when participants answered the open-ended questions of the survey. Some participants stated that they used social media to get ideas and inspiration for classroom setup and management, while other participants followed education blogs for the same reasons. All the participants who reported that they knew social media sites could be used for professional purposes stated in various ways that their professional use of social media focused on getting classroom ideas and collaborating with other educators.

Furthermore, participants were asked in the open-ended questions if they had explicit uses for specific social media sites. Each of the participants who chose to answer this question had very specific purposes for using each social media site. For example, many of the participants stated that the purpose of Pinterest was to gather (or pin) ideas focused on classroom setup and environment. Other participants stated that they use Teachers Pay Teachers to gain additional income or to buy center work.

Through the open-ended survey questions, participants also stated other purposes. Some participants used social media to stay connected to families. For example, one participant wrote, "I have a classroom Facebook page for parents only. I use this to post pictures and communicate what is going on in our classroom and building. Parents are not allowed to post on this site. Parents can private message me through Facebook with any questions or concerns." This also addressed the second theme of connections.

Connections

The second theme, connections, first became apparent when participants were asked, in an open-question format, to state their personal definition of social media (prior to reading the definition for the purpose of this study). All the responses indicated, either directly or indirectly, that participants defined social media as a resource to make connections.

As a reminder, the term "connection" is used in the definition of social media. This indicated to participants that social media is an avenue for connecting with other people, specifically fellow educators. For example, one participant wrote, "Anything that connects people to one another with the use of a technological device." Another participant wrote, "A place to publicly share thoughts and ideas with others."

Although the theme of connections first became apparent in the initial open-ended question, the idea of connections continued throughout the survey answers. In response to the most helpful portion of social media and the specific use of social media, many of the participants wrote about the fact that teachers can connect with each other and families through closed Facebook groups and sharing pictures through Shutterfly.

While reading the responses, the researcher found one response that addressed not only the idea of connections, but also the initial problem of teacher isolation. The participant wrote that the most helpful part of social media networking was that she was able to "connect with other teachers who teach my grade and have the same passion and values, which I might not find in my own building or district."

The idea of connecting and collaborating through technology supports the concept that social media can be used for more than a social, non-work-related tool; it can also be used as a tool to advance one's own network. Just as LinkedIn can be used to find connections, network, and advance a career, other social network platforms can be used in the same way, especially as people and tech companies continue to evolve and create uses for the technology that may not even be imagined yet.

Overwhelming

While many of the findings could directly link to both guiding research questions, the participants were specifically asked about the benefits and the pitfalls of social media networks for professional planning. The downfalls of social media, in the field of education, varied among the participants. Essentially, though, the participants felt there were too many options, creating a sense of being overwhelmed.

One participant summarized it best by stating that it was a "wealth of bad sources." Therefore, educators need to ensure that the material they are downloading, reading, or watching comes from a good source and will benefit them professionally; this process can be time-consuming and was recognized as such by the participants.

IMPLICATIONS

One implication from this study is the idea that teachers engage in social media to feel a sense of belonging and appreciation for the work they are doing in the classroom. As accountability measures continue to infiltrate into classrooms, teachers are feeling the strain. Teachers feel the pressure from their administrators, who feel the pressure from above, which is leading to a lack of motivation and sense of professionalism (Leithwood, Rosanne, & Jantzi, 2002). When teachers can build each other up using social media, validating each other, and increasing each other's dopamine levels by acknowledging ideas and teaching strategies, the teaching profession benefits.

Additionally, the findings from this study, in conjunction with other studies, lead to the assumption that teachers want to learn and interact. However, time constraints can prevent in-person interactions. The Internet, through the use of social media, is proving to be a beneficial way to plan, collaborate, and brainstorm with like-minded professionals. SME using SNSs is providing another way for teachers to reach each other when professional isolation is present.

DISCUSSION

The age of technology and social media is continually changing. Twenty years ago, people were just beginning to place computers in their homes for use. Ten years ago, people were beginning to communicate through other Internet-enabled devices. Then, the invention of social media sites arguably changed the way people communicate, both personally and professionally.

This research study investigated teachers' use of social media networks to plan, brainstorm, and collaborate to develop professionally. The findings point to the fact that professionally, teachers use social media with a purpose and feel a sense of connection in a profession of isolation. Social media and networking through social media continue to evolve, as does the profession of teaching.

While overarching themes were found and analyzed using the guiding research questions, further analysis brought into account the theory used in this study, the Social Media Engagement (SME) theory. As a reminder, the SME theory was developed by researchers who predicted "that the user experience, encompassing both the social interactions among users and the technical features of the social media platform, will influence user engagement" in a positive way (Di Gangi & Wasko, 2016, p. 2).

In other words, if the social media platform (i.e., Twitter or Facebook) is easy to use and there is positive feedback overall, then people (educators) are more likely to engage in knowledge-sharing communities through social media sites.

Overall, the participants in this study had positive feedback regarding the use of social media to plan, collaborate, and brainstorm. Teachers reported having positive feedback and therefore were able to grow and develop knowledge-sharing communities with professional goals in mind. This experience supports the scientific knowledge that when something is "liked," "shared," or otherwise recognized on social media, individuals receive a dopamine high, developing a sense of belonging (Soat, 2017). This sense of belonging creates an educational atmosphere where teachers are no longer teaching in isolation but are collaborating and communicating.

The outlined research, along with other scholarship focused on technology and communication, has both pros and cons. Pros include the ability to collaborate, save money, and interact with and learn from people all over the world. Cons include the lack of face-to-face communication, the fact that technology may not always work according to plan, and the presence of a generational divide focused on technology etiquette and knowledge creating an unequal field in the professional world. However, the world is becoming more technologically reliant, and as educators it is important that we understand the technology and the etiquette of having conversations and collaborations.

While the described research project was limited, it built the foundation for understanding how the education field uses technology to communicate. There are pros and cons, as outlined in Table 10.2. It is not an exhaustive list, but it is a list to begin the process of brainstorming.

Table 10.2. Educator's Professional Technology Use: Pros and Cons

\multicolumn{2}{c}{Professional Technology Use: Educators}	
Pros	Cons
Share knowledge and learn best teaching practices through videos or blogs.	Not all teachers have access or a means to access technology on a regular basis.
Build a network of like-minded individuals or individuals who share a career path.	Opens oneself up to the possibility of negative feedback.
	Too much is available on the Internet. Where is the validation or credibility? How do you know the information is accurate?

Epilogue

Excellent communication is an asset to every team, organization, school community, and relationship. While most of the research for communication techniques is based in the field of business, it is important for educators and administrators to develop a toolkit of resources and strategies to have professional conversations with colleagues, supervisors, and—arguably the most important groups—families and students.

From early childhood grades through secondary courses, educators need to develop professional skills to communicate effectively. Therefore, providing experiences, feedback, and coaching during the development of a professional communication toolkit is essential to the development of the whole educator. These discrete skills, such as reading social cues, developing comfortable eye contact, engaging in active listening, and so forth, are often overlooked or are not included as a focused skill in education programs or professional development in school districts (Graham-Clay, 2005). However, relationship building and communication are arguably the determining factors in home–school connections and a positive school culture.

As is evident in the information and tools provided in this book, there are multiple foundational pieces for prevention of and reaction to difficult conversations with multiple parties. Foundations for buildings are built with many blocks; likewise, our foundation for effective and respectful communication includes many foundation blocks.

References

Advanced Cardio Vascular Life Support (ACLS). 2018. Retrieved from https://acls.com/.

American Federation of Teachers. (2007). *Building parent-teacher relationships.* Washington, DC: American Federation of Teachers.

Anntar, A. (2018). 8 methods for effectively improving student communication skills. [Blog]. Retrieved from https://education.microsoft.com/Story/Lesson?token=NR3WV.

Australian Institute of Business (AIB). (2018). Communication blog. Retrieved from https://www.aib.edu.au/blog/communication/.

Brazelton, J., & Gorry, A. G. (2003). Creating a knowledge-sharing community: If you build it, will they come? *Communications of the ACM, 46*(2), 23–25.

Browning, D. M., Meyer, E. C., Truog, R. D., & Solomon, M. Z. (2009). Cultivating relational learning to address the hidden curriculum. Retrieved from https://mafiadoc.com/cultivating-relational-learning-to-address-the-hidden-curriculum_59b1e79f1723ddd8c6ad30d9.html.

Buehler, J., Ruggles Gere, A., Dallavis, C., & Shaw Haviland, V. (2009). Normalizing the fraughtness: How emotion, race, and school context complicate cultural competence. *Journal of Teacher Education, 60*(4), 408–418.

Businesstopia. (2018). Lasswell's communication model. Retrieved from https://www.businesstopia.net/communication/lasswell-communication-model.

Child Welfare Information Gateway. (2016). *Family engagement: Partnering with families to improve child welfare outcomes.* Washington, DC: U.S. Department of Health and Human Services, Children's Bureau.

Clarke, P. (2016). Motorcycle club gives allegedly bullied girl a ride to school. *ABC News*, May 26. Retrieved from https://abcnews.go.com/US/local-motorcycle-club-allegedly-bullied-girl-ride-school/story?id=39395162.

Communication Studies. (2019). Barriers to communication. [Blog]. Retrieved from http://www.communicationstudies.com/barriers-to-communication.

Datchuk, K. (2018). *Processing discomfort: Art, diversity, equity, and inclusion*. Presentation at Diversity in Education Conference, College of Education, University of Iowa.

Di Gangi, P. M., & Wasko, M. M. (2016). Social media engagement theory: Exploring the influence of user engagement on social media usage. *Journal of Organizational and End User Computing (JOEUC)*, *28*(2), 53–73.

Dieker, L., Hynes, M., Hughes, C., & Smith, E. (2008). Implications of mixed reality and simulation technologies on special education and teacher preparation. *Focus on Exceptional Children*, *40*(6), 1.

Doyle, A. (2018). Communication skills for workplace success. Retrieved from https://www.thebalancecareers.com/communication-skills-list-2063779.

Education World. (2016). Home visits forge school, family links. [Blog]. Retrieved from https://www.educationworld.com/a_admin/admin/admin342.shtml.

Ferlazzo, L. (2011). Involvement or engagement? *Schools, Families, and Communities*, *68*(8), 10–14.

Frey, C. (2010). Enhancing the learning opportunities through culturally responsive practices. *St. Mary College Rising Tide/Education Studies*, *3*.

Gay, G. (2000). *Culturally responsive teaching-theory, practice and pedagogy*. New York: Teachers College Press.

Ginopolis, M. (2011). Digitaleading - Part II. Big Think Blog. Retrieved from https://bigthink.com/digitaleading-part-ii.

Graham-Clay, S. (2005). Communicating with parents: Strategies for teachers. *School Community Journal*, *15*(1), 117–129.

Gray, C. (2018). Amputation, autism, and social stories. Retrieved from https://carolgraysocialstories.com/2018/01/16/amputation-autism-social-stories/.

Hardy, E. A. (2014). Teachers are doing it for themselves: Using social media for professional development and advocacy. *Forum: For Promoting 3–19 Comprehensive Education*, *56*(2), 265–276.

Henderson, A. T. (2011). *Family-school-community partnership 2.0.: Collaborative strategies to advance student learning*. Retrieved from https://www.nea.org/assets/docs/Family-School-Community-Partnerships-2.0.pdf.

Hendricks, D. (2013). Complete history of social media: Then and now. *Small Business Trends*. Retrieved from https://smallbiztrends.com/2013/05/the-complete-history-of-social-media-infographic.html.

Jantz, G. L. (2014). Brain differences between genders. Retrieved from https://www.psychologytoday.com/us/blog/hope-relationships/201402/brain-differences-between-genders.

Kabilan, M. K. (2016). Using Facebook as an e-portfolio in enhancing pre-service teachers' professional development. *Australasian Journal of Educational Technology*, *32*(1), 19–31.

Kankanhalli, A., Tan, B. C. Y., & Wei, K. K. (2005). Contributing knowledge to electronic knowledge repositories: An empirical investigation. *MIS Quarterly*, *29*(1), 113–143.

Khattak, S. R., Batool, S., Saleem, Z., & Takrim, K. (2016). Effects of social media on teachers' performance: Evidence from Pakistan. *Dialogue (Pakistan)*, *11*(2), 127–134.

Kio, S. I. (2015). Feedback theory through the lens of social networking. *Issues in Educational Research, 25*(2), 135–152. Retrieved from http://www.iier.org.au/iier25/kio.pdf.

Klein, C. (2013). Learning about communication blocks so parents can improve connection. [Blog]. Retrieved from https://bridges2understanding.com/learn-about-communication-blocks-so-parents-can-improve-connection/.

Krutka, D. G., & Carpenter, J. P. (2016). Participatory learning theory through social media: How and why social studies educators use twitter. *Contemporary Issues in Technology and Teacher Education, 16*(1), 38–59. Retrieved from https://citejournal.s3.amazonaws.com/wp-content/uploads/2016/05/v16i1socialstudies1.pdf.

Lasswell, H. (1948). The structure and function of communication in society. In L. Bryson (Ed.), *The communication of ideas*. New York: Harper.

Leithwood, K., Rosanne, K. L., & Jantzi, S. D. (2002). School leadership and teachers' motivation to implement accountability policies. *Education administration quarterly, 38*(1), 94–119.

Li, C., & Bernoff, J. (2008). *Groundswell: Winning in a world transformed by social technologies*. Boston, MA: Harvard Business School Press.

Lightfoot, S. (2004). *The essential conversation: What parents and teachers can learn from each other*. New York: Random House Publishing Company.

Lindsey, R. B., Roberts, L. M., & Campbell Jones, F. (2004). The culturally proficient school: An implementation guide for school leaders. Thousand Oaks, CA: Corwin Press.

McAnany, E. (2017). Wilbur Schramm. *Oxford Bibliographies*. Retrieved from http://www.oxfordbibliographies.com/view/document/obo-9780199756841/obo-9780199756841-0190.xml.

McLean, F. M., Dixon, R. M., & Verenikina, I. (2014). Bringing it to the teachers: Building a professional network among teachers in isolated schools. *Australian and International Journal of Rural Education, 24*(2), 15–22.

Meier, K. S. (2018). Gender barriers to communication. Retrieved from https://work.chron.com/gender-barriers-communication-6858.html.

Nambiar, R. M. K., & Thang, S. M. (2016). Examining Malaysian teachers' online blogs for reflective practices: Towards teacher professional development. *Language & Education: An International Journal, 30*(1), 43–57.

Osher, D., Sidana, A., & Kelly, P. (2008). *Improving conditions for learning for youth who are neglected or delinquent*. Washington, DC: American Institutes for Research, NDTAC. Retrieved from http://www.neglected-delinquent.org/nd/resources/spotlight/cflbrief200803.asp.

Overton, A. R., & Lowry, A. C. (2013). Conflict management: Difficult conversations with difficult people. *Clinics in Colon and Rectal Surgery, 26*(4), 259–264.

Pearson, J. C., & Nelson, P. E. (2000). *An introduction to human communication*. New York: McGraw-Hill.

Popkin, M. (2014). *Active parenting: A parent's guide to raising happy and successful children*. Marietta, GA: Active Parenting Publishers.

Prahalad, C. K., & Ramaswamy, V. (2004). *The future of competition: Co-creating unique value with customers*. Boston, MA: Harvard Business School Press.

Rozen, M. (2015). Courageous conversations: How to handle difficult conversations in the workplace and in our personal lives. Retrieved from https://www.huffingtonpost.com/michelle-rozen/courageous-conversations-_b_6446860.html.

Sarkis, S. A. (2017). *11 warning signs of gaslighting*. Psychology Today. [Blog]. Retrieved from https://www.psychologytoday.com/us/blog/here-there-and-everywhere/201701/11-warning-signs-gaslighting.

Satell, G. (2015). Why communication is today's most important skill. Retrieved from www.forbes.com.

Schneider, M. (2018). Most people handle difficult situations by ignoring them—and the fallout isn't pretty. Retrieved from https://www.inc.com/michael-schneider/70-percent-of-employees-avoid-difficult-conversations-their-companies-are-suffering-as-a-result.html.

Schramm, W. (1954). How communication works. In W. Schramm (Ed.), *The process and effects of mass communication*. Champaign, IL: University of Illinois Press.

Scott, S. (2004). *Fierce conversations: Achieving success at work and in life one conversation at a time*. New York: Berkley.

Shannon, C., & Weaver, W. (1949). *The mathematical theory of communication*. Champaign, IL: University of Illinois Press.

Soat, M. (2017). Social media triggers as dopamine high. *American Marketing Association*. Retrieved from https://www.ama.org/publications/MarketingNews/Pages/feeding-the-addiction.aspx.

Speak, H. (2014). Why is communication important to human life? Retrieved from https://www.hopespeak.com/blog/why-is-communication-important-to-human-life-2/.

Stevens, M. (2018). Starbucks C.E.O. apologizes after arrests of 2 Black men. *New York Times*, April 15. Retrieved from https://www.nytimes.com/2018/04/15/us/starbucks-philadelphia-black-men-arrest.html.

Stone, D., Patton, B., Heen, S., & Fisher, R. (2010). *Difficult conversations: How to discuss what matters most*. New York: Penguin Books.

Tahir, L., Thakib, M. T. M., Hamzah, M. H., Said, M. N. H. M., & Musah, M. B. (2017). Novice head teachers' isolation and loneliness experiences. *Educational Management Administration & Leadership, 45*(1), 164–189.

The College Board. (2004). Why is it important to communicate well? *Communication for business success*, v. 1.0, section 1.1.

Thompson, J. (2011). Beyond words. Retrieved from https://www.psychologytoday.com/us/blog/beyond-words/201109/is-nonverbal-communication-numbers-game.

Uplift Events. (2017). How to communicate effectively with your colleagues. [Blog]. Retrieved from https://www.upliftevents.com.au/blog/communicate-effectively-colleagues/. Verplaetses, L. S., Ferraro, M., & Anderberg, A. (2012). Collaboration cubed: Isolated mainstream teachers become ESL experts to school systems. *TESOL Journal, 3*(3), 350–372.

Wlodkowski, R. J., & Ginsberg, M. B. (1995). A framework for culturally responsive teaching. *Strengthening Student Engagement, 53*(1), 17–21.

Yale Poorvu Center for Teaching and Learning. (2018). Inclusive classroom climate. [Blog]. Retrieved from https://poorvucenter.yale.edu/ClassClimates.

Zakrzewski, V. (2012). Three ways administrators can foster teachers' growth. [Blog]. Retrieved from https://greatergood.berkeley.edu/article/item/3_ways_administrators_can_foster_teachers_growth.

About the Author

Dr. Anni K. Reinking has degrees in psychology, early childhood education, and curriculum and instruction. Dr. Reinking's research interests include play-based and developmentally appropriate practice in birth through second-grade classrooms, teacher preparation techniques, effective coaching and mentoring strategies, and multicultural education in early childhood classrooms.

www.ingramcontent.com/pod-product-compliance
Lightning Source LLC
Chambersburg PA
CBHW030146240426
43672CB00005B/286